THE NAACP

NAACP
JOIN!
GIVE!
ALSTON
NATIONWIDE MEMBERSHIP DRIVE
1909
NATIONAL ASSOCIATION FOR THE
ADVANCEMENT OF COLORED PEOPLE
20 WEST 40th STREET, NEW YORK 18, N.Y.
1949

AFRICAN-AMERICAN ACHIEVERS

THE NAACP

Darren Rhym

CHELSEA HOUSE PUBLISHERS
Philadelphia

Chelsea House Publishers
Editor in Chief Sally Cheney
Associate Editor in Chief Kim Shinners
Production Manager Pamela Loos
Art Director Sara Davis

The Chelsea House World Wide Web address is http://www.chelseahouse.com

Produced by Pre-Press Company, Inc., East Bridgewater, MA 02333

First Printing
1 3 5 7 9 8 6 4 2

Library of Congress Cataloging-in-Publication Data

Rhym, Darren.
The NAACP / Darren Rhym.
p. cm. —(African-Americans achievers)
Includes bibliographical references (p.).
ISBN 0-7910-5812-3 (alk. paper)—ISBN 0-7910-5813-1 (alk. paper)
1. National Association for the Advancement of Colored People—History—20th century. 2. African Americans—Civil rights—History—20th century. 3. African Americans—Legal status, laws, etc.—History—20th century. 4. United States—Race relations. I. Title: National Association for the Advancement of Colored People. II. Title. III. Series.

E185.5.N276 R49 2001
305.896'073'006073—dc21 00-065740

Frontispiece: *A recruiting poster celebrates the 40th anniversary of the National Association for the Advancement of Colored People (NAACP). Since its inception in 1909 the NAACP has worked to achieve equal educational, social, and political opportunities for all Americans—black and white.*

CONTENTS

AFRICAN-AMERICAN ACHIEVERS

The Black Cowboys

Black Filmmakers

The Black Muslims

Boyz II Men

The Buffalo Soldiers

The Harlem Globetrotters

The Harlem Renaissance

The History of the Black Church

The History of Gospel Music

The History of Motown

The History of Rap Music

The NAACP

The Negro Leagues

The Temptations

THE NAACP

1

The Great Accommodator and the Anti-Bookerites

"NO RACE CAN prosper 'til it learns that there is as much dignity in tilling a field as in writing a poem."
—Booker T. Washington

"The object of true education is not to make men carpenters but to make carpenters men."
—W. E. B. Du Bois

Booker T. Washington, (center) poses with the other founders of the Tuskegee Institute. Washington was an outspoken supporter of a moderate approach to the advancement of African Americans during the late 1800s. He believed that blacks could achieve civil rights through hard work and moral fortitude rather than by protest.

ON SEPTEMBER 18, 1895, a 39-year-old African American named Booker T. Washington stood before an audience of white men and women at the Cotton States and International Exposition in Atlanta, Georgia, and prepared to deliver a speech. Washington was understandably nervous: the exposition was a major event, planned by white organizers who aimed to prove to the world that the American South was no longer the "poor relation" of the North. The organizers had appealed to the U.S. Congress for federal assistance in 1894, and at the time they had invited Washington to speak before a congressional subcommittee with the hope that Republican committee members would be won over by black involvement in the project. Washington's appearance at the Atlanta Exposition was a reward of sorts for this cooperation.

Frederick Douglass's death in 1895 left a void in the leadership of the African-American community. One of the most influential advocates for black empowerment during both the Civil War and Reconstruction, his loss opened the door for W. E. B. Du Bois and Booker T. Washington to step into the forefront of black leadership.

The year 1895 marked a turning point in African-American history. Just seven months before the exposition, on February 20, Frederick Douglass—the most influential black man of the 19th century—had died, leaving most African Americans to wonder who would take his place as a representative of their race. Douglass's death was a blow to the cause of black freedom. In his 50 years as a political activist, he had founded an important antislavery newspaper (the *North Star*, later renamed *Frederick Douglass's Paper*), recruited black troops for the Union army during the Civil War, aided in the passage of the Fourteenth Amendment (which granted citizenship to blacks) and Fifteenth Amendment (which granted black men the right to vote) to the U.S. Constitution, and secured a series of federal appointments after the Reconstruction. One of his most eloquent and powerful statements was an 1892 attack on all Americans, northern and southern alike, for allowing the horrible crime of lynching to continue in the South. Risking the goodwill that blacks had established with northern states, Douglass accused northerners of complicity in the lynchings, declaring that "until the voice of the North shall be heard in emphatic condemnation and withering reproach against these continued ruthless mob-law murders, it will remain equally involved with the South in this common crime."

Booker T. Washington was an unlikely successor to the fiery Douglass. Dubbed the "Great Accommodator," Washington had a reputation for calling on blacks to act in moderation and to defer fighting for civil rights. For example, he urged black workers to remain in the South after the Civil War and contribute to the area's economic regrowth rather than migrate north or west in search of better jobs and equal treatment.

In 1881 Washington had established the Tuskegee Normal and Industrial Institute, an all-black college in Tuskegee, Alabama. From a dilapidated shanty and church, and with a limited staff, Washington built the institute into an important center for industrial education and economic advancement. He saw to it that the students of Tuskegee Institute learned self-help and self-reliance. In his autobiography, *Up from Slavery*, Washington relates that students not only erected most of the buildings on campus, but they also manufactured the bricks for the buildings. The school became known as the Tuskegee Machine, because many great skilled laborers and artisans trained there.

Washington strongly believed that the path to securing civil rights was through hard work, practical skills, moral uprightness, and thriftiness, rather than by protest and political activism. Bringing oneself out of poverty, he taught, was the key to equality for African Americans—and this required that blacks first learn to establish their own financial institutions and schools before they attempted to exercise their political rights. "Brains, property, and character for the Negro will settle the question of civil rights," Washington insisted. His public speeches on the subject drew a great deal of attention not only from fellow blacks but also from white business leaders, especially those in the South.

Now Washington stood before the crowd at the Atlanta Exposition and delivered this message once more. One of the most memorable passages in his speech was an impassioned call for blacks to work within existing conditions to raise themselves economically. He told a metaphorical tale of a ship in distress:

> A ship lost at sea for many days suddenly sighted a friendly vessel. From the mast of the unfortunate vessel was seen a signal, "Water, water; we die of thirst." The answer from the friendly vessel came back at once, "Cast down your bucket where you are." A second time the signal, "Water, water; send us water," ran up from the distressed vessel, and was answered, "Cast down your bucket where you are." . . . The captain of the distressed vessel, at last heeding the injunction, cast down his bucket, and it came up full of fresh, sparkling water from the mouth of the Amazon River. To those of my race who depend on bettering their condition in a foreign land or who underestimate the importance of cultivating friendly relations with the southern white man, who is their next-door neighbor, I would say, "Cast down your bucket where you are."

Washington approved of literacy and property requirements imposed on black voters, he said, because these limitations would force blacks to seek higher education and greater material riches. "In all things that are purely social, we can be as separate as the fingers," he declared, "yet one as the hand in all matters essential to progress." He downplayed the importance of cultural education for blacks, proclaiming that "[t]he opportunity to earn a dollar in a factory just now is worth infinitely more than the opportunity to spend a dollar in an opera house."

His words drew thunderous applause from the audience and cemented his position as the most powerful and influential black man in America. Newspapers throughout the country printed front-page stories of the address. Theodore Roosevelt, who would later be elected president of the United States, praised Washington as a "genius such as does not arise in a generation." The wealthy northern industrialist Andrew Carnegie called him "one of the most wonderful men living or who has ever lived."

The Great Accommodator's words did not elicit such enthusiasm from other groups, however. While the Atlanta speech ultimately led white leaders and most average blacks to accept Booker T. Washington as an almost official spokesperson for all African Americans, black intellectuals and political activists believed that Washington had betrayed his race by speaking out in support of Jim Crow laws—statutes first enacted in 1877 that essentially enforced racial segregation in the South. (The term "Jim Crow" came from the name of an offensive minstrel routine first performed in 1828 by Thomas Dartmouth "Daddy" Rice.) In reality, Booker T. Washington accepted such laws only in the short term, as a means to an end. He believed that they helped to remove distractions from the effort of improving the economic status of African Americans.

That wasn't how black intellectuals interpreted Washington's Atlanta speech. Newspaper publisher William Monroe Trotter was the first major figure to break from Booker T. Washington's "Atlanta Compromise." Trotter was a northerner, raised in a Boston, Massachusetts, suburb that was rich in abolitionist history. Many historians today consider him both a successor to the abolitionists, who in the mid-1800s labored to end slavery, and a predecessor to the civil rights crusaders of the 1950s and 1960s. Educated at Harvard, Trotter early in his career dedicated himself to repudiating Washington's philosophy. In 1901 he founded the *Boston Guardian*, which he modeled after the 1850 abolitionist newspaper the *Liberator*. The *Guardian's* message was one of absolute equality and of the passionate struggle to achieve it. But Trotter's uneven temperament prevented him from succeeding in unifying political forces against Washington.

That role fell instead to William Edward Burghardt (W. E. B.) Du Bois, who became the most prominent figure among the anti-Bookerites, as Washington's opponents came to be known. In 1903 Du Bois published *The Souls of Black Folk*, a collection of essays that profoundly affected the way American society viewed issues of racial equality, much as Harriet Beecher Stowe's novel *Uncle Tom's Cabin* had done more than 50 years earlier with the issue of slavery.

Du Bois fiercely opposed Washington's accommodationist thinking. "We have no right to sit silently by while the inevitable seeds are sown for a harvest of disaster to our children, black and white," he wrote. In this thinking Du Bois joined other black intellectuals and a group of whites known as "neo-abolitionists" (new abolitionists), many of whom were descendants of pre–Civil War campaigners against slavery. By the early 1900s, neo-abolitionists were growing increasingly distressed by the political status of African Americans, and so they helped organize and fund a new movement that gave fresh momentum to the push for equality.

Booker T. Washington had led African Americans to a crossroads. He did not believe Du Bois could ever understand the complex plight of the Southern black man because he was not himself a Southerner. Du Bois believed that Washington was asking blacks to relinquish their integrity by remaining dependent upon whites. His public clashes with Booker T. Washington are well documented in *The Souls of Black Folk*, in which he directly challenges the latter's accommodationist theories. He writes that he wishes it were "possible for a man to be both a Negro and an American, without being cursed and spit upon by his fellows, without having the doors of Opportunity closed roughly in his face."

Du Bois's battle with Washington quickly became a philosophical and social debate over how blacks would achieve equal footing with whites. It included broad and ardent disputes over radical versus conservative behavior, over whether social equality can be achieved through economic success, and over segregation. It pitted intellectuals, who generally sided with Du Bois, against laborers, who more often agreed with Washington.

Fueled by these open and passionate debates, the new movement spawned by blacks such as W. E. B. Du Bois and by white neo-abolitionists ultimately evolved into the National Association for the Advancement of Colored People (NAACP). The long, proud, and often controversial history of the NAACP is a story of just such debates, and it continues with great vigor and spirit today.

2

"Hammering at the Truth": The Niagara Movement

UNLIKE BOOKER T. WASHINGTON, W. E. B. Du Bois believed that African-American freedom could be obtained only via the ballot—and that academic education was the key to this power. "The training of the schools we need to-day more than ever," he wrote, "above all the broader, deeper, higher culture of gifted minds and pure hearts. The power of the ballot we need in sheer self-defense—else what shall save us from a second slavery?"

Washington and Du Bois were a study in contrasts. Washington had been born a slave in Virginia in the late 1850s, and he took pride in being a "self-made man." He believed that to earn respect from whites, blacks needed to prove themselves as reliable and hard workers, and they had to demonstrate loyalty to white employers by abstaining from forming or joining unions and from crossing picket lines. For the sake of their own long-term political benefit, Washington believed, blacks should accept whatever wages they could get, even if they were far lower than that of white counterparts. His principles persuaded millions of black laborers to remain in the South and earned him the gratitude and financial support of many Southern white business leaders.

W. E. B. Du Bois, one of the primary organizers of the Niagara Movement, called its first gathering "one of the greatest meetings the American Negroes have ever held." The Niagara Movement included many individuals who later played an integral role in the creation of the NAACP.

Initially, Du Bois's philosophy of political activism, his theory of economic and academic independence from whites, and his belief in restoring African-American pride and self-worth were considered radical. He believed that whites, who had kidnapped blacks from Africa, enslaved them, and then been forced to free them but offered no remuneration for their skills, now had a duty and responsibility to remedy their transgressions. In stark contrast to Washington, he distrusted Southern whites and did not believe they had the best interests of his race at heart. It was clear to Du Bois that African-American workers had few rights in the South. There was no recourse against this discrimination, no group to organize them or champion their rights, no labor unions, and few laws to protect them. Despite the ratification of the Fourteenth Amendment in 1868 and the Fifteenth Amendment in 1870, African Americans had suffered a steady decline in political fortunes in the decades leading to the turn of the 20th century.

In the post–Civil War era known as Reconstruction, African Americans found themselves in a familiar situation. Although the war had bought their freedom, they were still relegated to sharecropping and renting, rather than having the economic freedom to own property and homes. African-American farmers contributed to the industrial expansion of the South, yet they did not benefit from it the way most whites did.

Before they lost power completely, blacks attempted a political comeback in the early 1890s by affiliating themselves with a movement known as populism, a third-party group that emerged as a savior to small farmers struggling with falling agricultural prices and rising debt. Populists called for banking reforms, government ownership of railroads, and a graduated income tax. They believed that the farmers' troubles derived from placing too much capital and power in the hands of corporations. Big business,

Although the Civil War resulted in blacks receiving their freedom from slavery, conditions changed very little in the South. Many blacks continued to live in poverty while working for extremely low wages in white-owned factories or farms.

they believed, had corrupted the democratic process, and they demanded political reform.

Southern Populists concentrated on taking back political power from plantation owners, merchants, and industrialists. In 1886 an organization called the Colored Farmers Alliance, a mirror group of the whites-only Southern Farmers' Alliance, was instituted to help blacks earn higher prices for their goods by selling them collectively. Internal conflicts caused the alliance to collapse just five years later, but in 1892, when the Populist movement became a political organization, it began reaching out to black politicians and voters. Ninety blacks served as delegates to the party's first national convention that year.

In the long run, however, the Populist alliance among blacks and whites did not last. Many blacks

Because Abraham Lincoln and his newly formed Republican political party had opposed slavery during the Civil War, many blacks remained loyal to the Republican Party in the years after the war.

continued to support the Republicans, and many of those who did back the Populists were intimidated by Democrat campaigns attempting to force them to vote Democratic. Realizing that they were losing black votes to their opponents, white Populists ultimately turned on blacks, viewing them as betrayers. Many of these Populists became the strongest proponents of segregation laws and of constitutional amendments restricting black voting. The ironic result was that the political party that once appeared to offer the most hope for demolishing Jim Crow laws ended up accelerating the process of passing such restrictions.

Perhaps more devastating to blacks than being disenfranchised from the Populist Party were several

Supreme Court decisions that caused severe setbacks in the push for black equality. In the first, an 1890 Mississippi poll tax and literacy requirement was upheld. Since illiteracy was high among Southern blacks after the Civil War—it had been illegal for slaves to learn to read and write—this ruling effectively excluded blacks from voting. The Court's most dangerous decision for African Americans, however, was the 1896 *Plessy v. Ferguson* ruling, in which the Supreme Court declared that it was legal to socially separate African Americans from whites as long as their segregated conditions and facilities were "equal."

By the early 20th century the erosion of black political influence was nearly complete. In 1901, for example, African Americans were eliminated from the U.S. Congress when North Carolinian George White lost his seat. (Twenty-eight years passed before another black would be elected to the federal legislature.) In 1902, only 5,000 blacks in Louisiana and only 3,000 in Alabama were eligible to vote. Racism dominated nearly every aspect of American society during this period. Scholars justified the inferior social status of African Americans in writings purporting that blacks were happiest under the slave system and were "lost" without the guidance of their masters. "Biologists" cited cases they claimed could prove that African Americans were one step removed from a species of ape. Some white religious leaders argued that the poor and downtrodden (including most Southern blacks) were being punished for their "imperfect souls." The concept of African Americans as second-class citizens had been reinforced by social and natural scientists, by theologians, by state legislatures, even by the highest court in the country.

While Booker T. Washington still argued that blacks were not yet fully prepared to exercise their political rights, Du Bois grew tired of "waiting" for black acceptance. He firmly believed that social equality and the right to vote were immediate and important requirements to achieving full citizenship. The Niagara Movement was his first attempt at achieving that goal.

In July 1905, Du Bois, William Monroe Trotter, and a group of disenchanted young African Americans met at Niagara Falls for three days of discussion. (They were forced to meet on the Canadian side of the falls because no hotel on the American side would accept black guests.) The purpose of the meeting was to create an organization that would take aggressive action to secure full citizenship for blacks. The participants in what would become known as the Niagara Movement believed that the time for compromise and compliance was over. They considered themselves at war, and they decided to fight to the finish.

The group drew up a platform for action. Du Bois thought that the best way to counter Washington's accommodationism was with what he termed "ceaseless agitation and insistent demand for equality [involving] the use of force of every sort: moral suasion, propaganda and where possible even physical resistance." For him, it was especially imperative that African Americans achieve social and political integration and procure higher education for the "Talented Tenth" of the African-American population, a percentage that he called "group leaders." He envisioned such a leader as one who established "the ideals of the community where he lives, directs its thoughts and heads its social movements."

During the 1905 meeting the Niagara founders agreed to hold annual conferences at which they would issue regular declarations of protest to white America—and they decided to choose meeting sites of significant importance to the struggle for black freedom. On August 15, 1906, the Niagarites, as they called themselves, convened at Harpers Ferry, Virginia (now West Virginia). There, in 1859, aboli-

THE STORMING OF THE ENGINE-HOUSE BY THE UNITED STATES MARINES.—[SKETCHED BY PORTE CRAYON.]

tionist John Brown, who had aided antislavery forces in Kansas and had been involved in the Underground Railroad out of Missouri, launched an armed assault on the U.S. arsenal and was captured and hanged.

More than 100 delegates turned out for the 1906 Harpers Ferry gathering, which Du Bois called "one of the greatest meetings that American Negroes have ever held." The participants, he said, "talked some of the plainest English that has been given voice to by black men in America." The Niagarites issued demands on burning issues in America, including freedom of speech and criticism, "full manhood suffrage" (the right to vote, given only to men—women would not achieve suffrage until 1920), the abolition of all distinctions based on race, the recognition of the basic principles of human fellowship, and respect for the working class. They wanted improvements in educational facilities, the integration of public

One of the first meeting sites of the Niagara Movement was Harpers Ferry, West Virginia. It was at Harpers Ferry that abolitionist John Brown, in 1859, captured a U.S. arsenal to obtain arms needed to free slaves. Brown's attempt was a failure and he was captured and hanged for treason.

facilities, and "the right of freemen to walk, talk, and be with them that wish to be with us." For those who did not agree, the Niagarites had strong words:

> We want the laws enforced against rich as well as poor; against capitalists as well as laborers; against white as well as black. We are not more lawless than the white race, [but] we are more often arrested, convicted and mobbed. We want the Constitution of the country enforced. . . .
>
> We want the Fourteenth Amendment carried out to the letter and every state disfranchised in Congress which attempts to disfranchise its rightful voters. We want the Fifteenth Amendment enforced and no state allowed to base its franchise simply on color. . . . How shall we get them? By voting where we may vote; by persistent, unceasing agitation; hammering at the truth; by sacrifice and work.

The members of the Niagara Movement drew up a "Declaration of Principles," a set of standards for governing the organization and addressing its issues and concerns. The declaration made clear that fierce condemnation was at the heart of the movement. "The Negro race in America, stolen, ravished, and degraded, struggling up through difficulties and oppression, needs sympathy and receives criticism, needs help and is given hindrance, needs protection and is given mob-violence, needs justice and is given charity, needs leadership and is given cowardice and apology, needs bread and is given a stone," Du Bois and Trotter wrote. "This nation will never stand justified before God until these things are changed."

Women were an important topic at the Niagarites' meeting as well. Trotter had always stiffly opposed the admission of women, but Du Bois overruled his objection and forced the issue by organizing, on his own authority, a Massachusetts Niagara Women's Auxiliary. Eventually women were offi-

Booker T. Washington took offense to the Niagara Movement's support of philosophies that conflicted with his own opinion on how African-Americans should best approach becoming equal members of society. He went to great lengths to discredit the movement, disrupting meetings and limiting its exposure in the press.

cially invited to join the main organization. *New York Evening Post* reporter Mary White Ovington, a white liberal, attended the Harpers Ferry meeting not only to record the events but also as an admirer of Du Bois's work and career. The two had first met in 1904 and began corresponding; while Ovington relied on his advice regarding the issues facing African Americans, she provided him with the means to secure a broader audience. It was she who first suggested that he invite her to the Niagara meeting; thereafter she joined the movement as its only white member and was heavily involved in civil rights activities.

At the end of the conference, the movement issued an "Address to the Country," penned by Du Bois, in which it demanded an end to segregation, racial violence, and the disenfranchisement of blacks. It demanded equal access to education, equal economic opportunity, equal treatment in the courts, the elimination of caste (social) distinctions based on race, recognition of the basic principles of brotherhood, and respect for the laborer. Du Bois ended the address with these moving words: "We claim ourselves every single right that belongs to a freeborn American, political, civil and social; and until we get these rights we will never cease to protest and to assail the ears of America. The battle we wage is not for ourselves alone but for all true Americans."

For five years the Niagara Movement experienced modest success, but with success came great difficulties. The third Niagara meeting, held in the abolitionist landmark city of Boston, Massachusetts, was marred by infighting between Trotter and fellow Niagarite Clement Garnett Morgan. Although Du Bois forged a temporary truce between the two, it did not last long. After a series of disagreements involving the state governor's election, Trotter's wife abruptly quit the movement. Du Bois refused to give in to Trotter's 22-page list of demands, in which Trotter objected to former colleague George Forbes's help and Morgan's extensive role in planning the Boston conference. The rift never fully mended. In addition, Booker T. Washington, angered by the group's challenge to his policy of accommodation, began launching schemes to discredit the Niagarites and to disrupt their meetings. He even went so far as to pay black newspapers not to report on the Niagara Movement's activities and accomplishments, and he hired agents to infiltrate the meetings on his behalf.

When the fourth meeting convened in Oberlin, Ohio, in 1908, Du Bois realized that the Niagara Movement was struggling. Part of the reason for its demise the following year was its reluctance to cultivate white allies and its failure to appeal to the black masses. It also insisted on ideological conformity among its members, and did not accept deviations from its strong radical stance. In contrast, Booker T. Washington's accommodationist philosophy led him to accept support from anyone who was willing to provide it, regardless of race, class, or political conviction.

In the end, the Niagara Movement did produce some tangible results. Local chapters in Chicago, Illinois, and Philadelphia, Pennsylvania, helped resist school segregation in those cities. It legally forced a northern railroad company to eliminate segregation in its passenger trains. More broadly—and most importantly—it was the first African-American institution dedicated solely to protesting racial oppression. It inspired people like Robert Abbott of Chicago, formerly an accommodationist, to launch vehicles of protest such as the *Defender*, a black newspaper that became known as the most militant and distinguished publication of its kind. It united many blacks across the country in a spirit of strong protest, and ultimately paved the way for even stronger movements and more substantial progress in establishing racial equality.

3

The Birth of the NAACP

Mary White Ovington (left) speaks with Mamie Davis of the NAACP's housing committee. In many ways Ovington can be seen as the founder of the NAACP. Moved by the violence against blacks, she looked to form an organization specifically focused on the protection of black rights.

TODAY, THE NAACP is not only the oldest and largest civil rights organization in the United States, but it is also viewed as the strongest. Unlike the short-lived Niagara Movement, the NAACP's long history includes the cooperative efforts of blacks and whites during periods when such unions were unpopular and were even considered "disloyal" to the cause.

The NAACP was born of violence. A race riot that broke out on August 14, 1908, in Springfield, Illinois—Abraham Lincoln's hometown—was the motivation for creating the organization. Springfield's population was 90 percent white, although the African-American population was growing as newcomers arrived to work in the mines and on the rails. The influx of blacks had created a simmering racial tension in the town. The spark was ignited when a white railwayman alleged that his wife had been raped by a young African American named George Richardson. The sheriff arranged to have the alleged rapist removed from the Springfield prison "to save his life." The decision outraged many of the white townspeople.

"What the hell are you fellas afraid of?" an angry white woman yelled as the lawmen removed

Richardson. Cries of "Women want protection!" rang out, and an angry crowd of street railwaymen who had gathered at the prison were incited to violence. In the ensuing riot, more than 80 were injured. Six blacks were fatally shot and two were lynched. More than $200,000 in damage was sustained, and before militiamen could restore order 2,000 African Americans had fled the area in terror.

The Niagara Movement issued a biting condemnation of the riot and publicly "cursed" what it identified as the "Negro haters of America." By this time, however, the movement was foundering, so it had nothing with which to back its powerful words. Many members of the white liberal press were shocked and disturbed by news of the Springfield riot. Oswald Garrison Villard, head of the *New York Evening Post* and grandson of abolitionist William Lloyd Garrison, traveled to Springfield with William English Walling, a wealthy reporter and socialist from Kentucky, to investigate the riot. Afterward, in an article for the *Independent* entitled "The Race War in the North," Walling vividly described the gruesome details of the lynchings and condemned the public for ignoring such atrocities against blacks. He openly questioned whether or not democracy could survive if this kind of lawlessness continued.

Mary White Ovington read William Walling's article and was moved to action. In the first week of January 1909, Ovington and Walling met at Walling's Manhattan apartment with Dr. Henry Moscowitz, a liberal social worker, to discuss founding an organization that would fight for black rights throughout America. Ovington and Walling invited Oswald Garrison Villard to be one of the first members; soon others, including Bishop Walters, the first African American to join, were also invited. In an announcement to publicize the inaugural meeting, Oswald Villard wrote, "We call upon all believers in democracy to join in a national conference for the discussion of present evils, the voicing of protests, and the renewal of the struggle for civil and political liberty."

On February 12, 1909, the 100th anniversary of Abraham Lincoln's birth, the National Negro Conference gathered for its first meeting. Except William Monroe Trotter (who declined to participate because, he said, he mistrusted white people), all the major figures of the Niagara Movement attended. Discussions that day centered on the same issues that concerned the Niagarites: suffrage for blacks, an end to segregation and racial violence, and the need for effective academic programs for blacks. By the close of the conference, the members had drawn up a formal plan of action and agreed to establish a permanent organization to fulfill their plan.

The delegates agreed to hold a "Conference on the Status of the Negro" beginning on May 31 of that year. Among the 1,000 people they invited to attend were a number of prominent whites, many of whom were descendants of abolitionists. The organizers also invited the two most influential African Americans of the time: Booker T. Washington and W. E. B. Du Bois. Despite Washington's prominence, organizers were divided about inviting him. White liberals and many blacks had grown upset and impatient with Washington's philosophies, and most of them endorsed Du Bois's strategy of protest and agitation instead.

Booker T. Washington had suffered a number of setbacks to his policies during this period of increased violence against blacks. It had become abundantly clear to white organizers of the conference—and to other white liberals—that accommodationism was not the solution to the problem of African-American oppression in the United States. Although blacks were making strides educationally and financially, as Washington's philosophy advocated, they were also steadily losing ground socially and politically. Cooperation with powerful Southern white moderates, once the source of strength for Washington, no longer seemed to be a productive or acceptable strategy.

At the turn of the 20th century, Booker T. Washington had the power to make or break the careers of prominent blacks. American presidents consulted him on matters of race, and he all but controlled the philanthropic moneys assigned to African-American causes. For many years, Washington tried to persuade Du Bois to join his cause, in part because he did not want Du Bois as an adversary. As Du Bois grew disenchanted with Washington's accommodationist views, however, he began establishing himself as a strong leader in his own right.

Du Bois's popularity soared after he helped found the Niagara Movement. Mary White Ovington, who had attended the 1906 annual meeting of the Niagara Movement, had the same year attended a meeting of Washington's Negro Business League. She came away clearly sympathizing with Du Bois, and her support of his views seemed to reflect that of most white liberals who became involved in the cause. In this way, Du Bois achieved a kind of symbolic victory over Washington.

African Americans were not the catalysts in creating the National Negro Conference; but if Mary Ovington and William English Walling were the sparks of the organization, and Oswald Villard was one of the engines, it was W. E. B. Du Bois who fueled the conference and gave it energy. Several factors kept Du Bois from being more deeply involved in the early stages of establishing the National Negro Conference. One was his commitment to continue teaching at Atlanta University in Georgia, where he was an instructor. Moreover, his limited funds prevented him from frequent travel to New York, where the organizers lived and the headquarters was eventually established. Still, without Du Bois's backing, especially on issues of education for African Americans,

James Weldon Johnson, once a devoted follower of Booker T. Washington, became a branch organizer for the NAACP and was the organization's first African-American executive secretary.

the organization would have lacked legitimacy and might not have been taken seriously.

Villard invited Booker T. Washington to the 1909 meeting of the National Negro Committee as a formality, but most of the members hoped that he would decline the invitation. The decision not to include Washington as a full participant in the conference was one that Ovington did not take lightly. She agonized over the question of whether it was possible to build an organization that addressed the needs and concerns of African Americans without the strong support and sanction of Washington. In her book *Black and White Sat Down Together*, Ovington explains the motivation for excluding from the conference the "most influential and most famous Negro living":

> I thought then, and I still think, that Washington would not have come in with us if he had been asked. Of course, he could have joined the committee to kill it, but, if he was like every other Negro I knew, he would have rejoiced at the thought that there was a group of people, of both races, prepared to battle for the Negroes' rights. And what I felt keenly was that, if we put on his name, we should not have the support of the Negroes whom we absolutely needed. We would start out under suspicion.

Nearly 300 people attended the May 31, 1909, meeting of the National Negro Committee. The attendees included prominent philosophers, anthropologists, educators, and economists, all of whom held the goal of improving the lives of African Americans. Together, they decided to create a permanent organization, complete with a publicity bureau and press section, a legal committee, a political bureau, a civil rights commission, an education department, an industrial bureau, and an overseeing board (named the Committee of Forty). This last group was assigned to continue the work that the National Negro Committee had begun at the conference.

Ovington believed that important national work would quickly present itself, but unfortunately the young organization was hampered by a lack of funds, and therefore it was not in a position to handle such work immediately. Under the skillful management of Committee of Forty executive secretary Frances Blascoer, however, the National Negro Committee had held four mass meetings, distributed thousands of pamphlets, and numbered their membership in the many hundreds by the end of 1909.

On May 5, 1910, at a final planning meeting for the National Negro Committee's second annual conference, the participants voted to change the name of the organization to the National Association for the Advancement of Colored People. The newly named organization would consist of a national committee of 30, with headquarters in New York City. The planners worked out other details, such as membership costs and issues to be discussed at meetings. The activities of the NAACP would include providing legal aid, organizing mass meetings, investigating injustices, and establishing a publicity campaign to promote their causes.

After these details were worked out, the NAACP chose its leaders. With the help of Villard and Ovington, the transition went smoothly. Moorfield Storey, a white lawyer from Boston with many years of service in black causes, was named the first NAACP president. Ovington was named secretary, Walter Sachs was named treasurer, Walling became the chairman of the executive committee, and Villard was named assistant (disbursing) treasurer.

Ovington considered "the securing of a sufficient financial support to warrant our calling Dr. Du Bois from Atlanta University into an executive office" the most critical work of the conference members. Ultimately, Du Bois did leave his teaching position at Atlanta University and was brought on as a paid chairman of the NAACP executive committee, thus becoming the only African American on the committee. Within weeks, the position of chairman of the executive committee was split: Frances Blascoer assumed all of the administrative responsibilities, while Du Bois focused on publicity and research.

In November 1910, Du Bois published the first issue of the group's newspaper, *The Crisis* (a title derived from poet James Russell Lowell's "The Present Crisis"). Soon after Du Bois's appointment, 14 former members of the Niagara Movement also joined the NAACP committee. As the NAACP grew, Booker T. Washington's comments on the organization, at first polite and restrained, became critical and angry. Eventually he began using pressure to disrupt the organization, just as he had done with the Niagara Movement. He called on reporters loyal to his camp to find and publish unfavorable information on white liberal members as a means of harassing them. The NAACP was much stronger than the Niagara Movement had been, and Washington's attacks did little damage. Nevertheless, until his death in 1915, Booker T. Washington vehemently opposed the activities of the NAACP.

Washington's followers ultimately made peace with the NAACP. After the Great Accommodator's death, Du Bois suggested that the association invite Bookerites to a "reconciliation conference" in Amenia, New York. From this successful meeting came many new NAACP members, including James Weldon Johnson, a lawyer who had been an American consul in Venezuela and Nicaragua. Formerly a strong Bookerite, by the end of 1916 Johnson was an NAACP branch organizer and had become the first black executive secretary of the organization—a position he held until 1931, seven years before his death.

The creation of the NAACP was a painstaking and delicate process. From the very beginning, black organizers who were invited to participate understandably distrusted the white liberals who made up the majority of its members. Organizers like Mary Ovington largely understood this distrust. Like the other white members, she knew the painful history of the African-American struggle for equal rights—but she also knew that she and the other whites in the organization were genuine in their efforts to effect change. Charles Edward Russell clearly shared Ovington's hope and optimism that all of them, black and white, would succeed:

> I can't think we have had too much agitation. I have had more education on this question since 10 o'clock this morning than I have had before in all the rest of my life, and I think I have been a pretty close observer. I tell you that what I have heard today has opened up an entirely new horizon to me. . . . Now there are only a few of us here, but it is a beginning and every great movement has to have its beginning, and if we still strike hands together and increase our numbers and look forward, we will have our remedy.

THE CRISIS

A RECORD OF THE DARKER RACES

Volume One — NOVEMBER, 1910 — Number One

Edited by W. E. BURGHARDT DU BOIS, with the co-operation of Oswald Garrison Villard, J. Max Barber, Charles Edward Russell, Kelly Miller, W. S. Braithwaite and M. D. Maclean.

CONTENTS

PUBLISHED MONTHLY BY THE

National Association for the Advancement of Colored People

AT TWENTY VESEY STREET — NEW YORK CITY

ONE DOLLAR A YEAR — TEN CENTS A COPY

4

The Crisis

DESPITE THE FACT that white activists played essential roles in creating and contributing to the NAACP, some African Americans grew increasingly uneasy about white control of an organization that was meant for the betterment of African-American lives. After all, they reasoned, who knew better what was best for blacks than blacks themselves?

These differences came to the surface as early as the founding conference in May 1909, when Ida Wells-Barnett openly expressed concern over the leading roles whites were playing in the movement. Both she and William Monroe Trotter shied away from deep involvement in the new organization for this reason. Black resentment about white control was also evident in the frequent clashes between W. E. B. Du Bois and Oswald Garrison Villard.

The cover of the first issue of The Crisis, *edited by W. E. B. Du Bois.* The Crisis *is one of the longest-running publications created for and by African Americans.*

Du Bois especially resented the intrusion of whites into the editorial affairs of *The Crisis*, which he maintained as an independent publication. Originally titled *The Crisis: A Record of the Darker Races*, the paper was meant to be the "chronicler of African-American history, thought, and culture." While the newspaper was established as the voice of the NAACP, it had its own separate staff of 8 to 10 people. Many white members, however, felt that *The Crisis* did not report NAACP news sufficiently. They believed that Du Bois's denunciations of whites in the paper were inflammatory, and that his edito-rial style was "propagandistic and unbalanced," especially since he refused to cover negative topics such as crime committed by blacks.

Du Bois argued that his purpose in publishing *The Crisis* was "to set forth those facts and arguments which show the danger of race prejudice, particularly as manifested today toward colored people. It takes its name from the fact [that] the editors believe that this is a critical time in the history of the advancement of men." The monthly issues included literature (such as poems and short stories), editorial commentary, feature articles, reports of NAACP activities, and discussions of current events of interest to African Americans. Two regular features in the early days of *The Crisis* were "American Negroes in College" and "Along the NAACP Battlefront."

Du Bois intended *The Crisis* to fulfill several functions. First and most important, he said, it was a record of "very important happenings and movement in the world which bears on the great problem of interracial relations and especially those which affect the Negro-American." Second, the newspaper served as a comprehensive review "of opinion and literature" pertinent to the race problem. Third, it was a vehicle for his own editorials regarding the issues facing African Americans. On the editorial page, Du Bois declared that he stood "for the rights of men, irrespective of color or race, [and] for the highest ideals of American democracy."

In addition to the editorial section, the paper also contained "Along the Color Line," which covered briefs on politics, education, social uplift, organizations and meetings, science, and art. The "Opinion" section provided a forum for representative views on

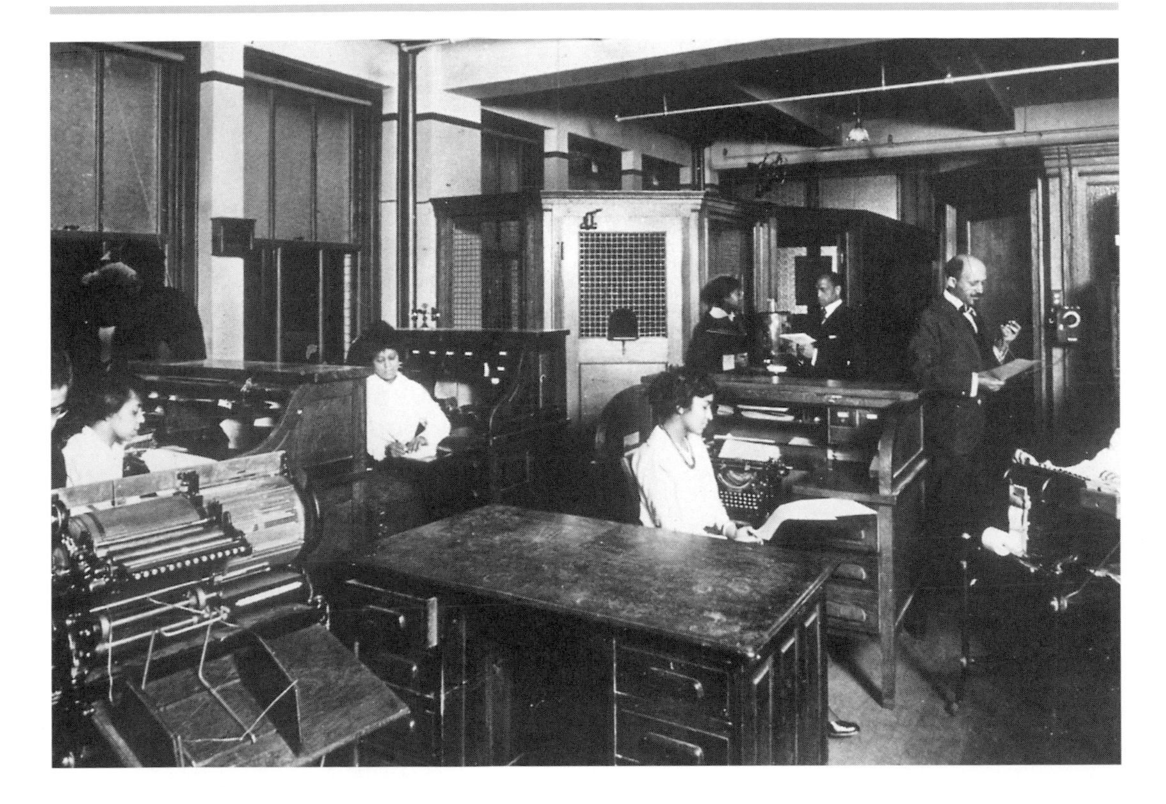

W. E. B. Du Bois (far right) looks over his work, surrounded by his staff in The Crisis *offices. The publication was a huge success, selling close to 350,000 copies in its first two years of existence.*

important questions of the day from well-known African-American leaders. Another section, "The Burden," was reserved for reporting civil, economic, political, and other atrocities perpetrated against African Americans. "What to Read," which appeared in the first issue as a simple list of titles, later evolved into a regular collection of concise reviews of magazine articles and books that focused on issues concerning blacks around the world. In the year after its first appearance *The Crisis* also launched two more sections: "Talks About Women," which contained information about the women's suffrage movement (in which Du Bois was involved) and "Men of the Month," which featured profiles of prominent black leaders in the movement.

The early success of *The Crisis* was phenomenal. The first printing of just 1,000 copies sold out immediately, so Du Bois doubled the number of pages in the publication and printed 2,500 copies of the second issue. By March 1911—just four months after its launch—the print run was up to 6,000. Most of the major black colleges and universities, including Atlanta, Fisk, Howard, Shaw, Virginia Union, and Wilberforce, joined the growing list of advertisers. (Two notable universities, Hampton and Tuskegee, were not among the backers because of their affiliation with and loyalty to Booker T. Washington.)

In April 1912, the circulation of *The Crisis* reached an astounding 22,500. The paper's year-end financial statement submitted to the NAACP treasurer reported a total of 350,000 copies sold from November 1910 to November 1912, generating an income of $17,374.51—an impressive figure, until $17,132.03 in expenses was deducted, leaving the paper with a balance of just $242.48. Undeterred, Du Bois calculated that the newspaper's future would be secure when its circulation reached 50,000 subscribers. For a $2 membership in the association or 10 cents per issue of *The Crisis*, subscribers received exceptional value.

The cost of success for *The Crisis* was dear, however. Du Bois and his paper made many enemies. Not only did *The Crisis* continue to attack Du Bois's favorite target, Booker T. Washington, but it also went after Wilberforce University, a historically black school, for "falling almost hopelessly behind the trends" in providing quality education. *The Crisis* also attacked broader institutions such as the black church, which Du Bois believed had become "choked with pretentious ill-trained men and in far too many cases with men dishonest or otherwise immoral." He believed that the church was too caught up in trying to keep people from doing things it believed were sinful (such as dancing and theatergoing) and in placing blame on educated blacks who objected to "silly empty sermons." Du Bois railed at black church leaders who seemed unconcerned with the real issues facing members of their congregations.

Du Bois also assaulted the powerful and well-established black press, so much so that the *Bee*, a Washington, D.C., newspaper, mocked *The Crisis* and its editor, calling them the "catspaws of arrogant, powerful whites." Du Bois counterattacked by labeling the *Bee* and the black press in general anti-intellectuals, stating that they were just "plain bad at grammar." He challenged other black newspapers and magazines to cover events "other than weddings and murders."

As the barrage of hostile editorials aimed at Du Bois continued, the NAACP's white officials became extremely concerned. The *Bee* criticized Du Bois's "Harvardized English." The Richmond *Planet* advised its readers to ignore the "professional bookworm." Other members of the black press blamed Du Bois for having seriously "damaged his own cause." Talk surfaced that perhaps Du Bois had become deranged and that his brilliant mind had grown "undoubtedly warped." As a result, the NAACP began distancing itself from *The Crisis*, and it took pains to praise the black press at its annual conference in 1914.

Clearly, W. E. B. Du Bois had become synonymous with *The Crisis*. He had never been known as a "mixer" or joiner, so he had never seriously considered leading the NAACP. He knew he would not be popular in such a position and insisted that he simply wanted to be left alone to manage *The Crisis*. Rather than seeing himself as an officer of the organization, Du Bois considered himself an "intellectual turned propagandist." *The Crisis* soon became a paradox: a self-financed publication meant to represent a larger organization, but led by a militant editor with whom his colleagues believed they could not reason or argue.

NAACP officials had naturally assumed that Du Bois would merely advance the policies of the organization, which were guided by the careful decisions of the 30-member board of directors on which he sat. From the start, however, Du Bois was skeptical over whether white officers could be trusted to make decisions that were in the best interest of African Americans. Before long, he began viewing himself as indispensable to the NAACP's success, and thus he interpreted any attempt at interfering with his editorial role as a racist or perverse attack.

One example of the dilemma this attitude raised occurred when NAACP chairman Oswald Garrison Villard admitted that he thought the reporting in *The Crisis* was unbalanced. He suggested to Du Bois that the newspaper remedy the situation by regularly publishing a list of crimes committed by African Americans. Du Bois flatly refused, informing the chairman that he did not consider himself the chairman's "subordinate," but rather a "fellow officer" and therefore not required to carry out his request.

The issue grew so heated that the NAACP board eventually convened to settle the dispute between Villard and Du Bois. Keenly aware of the political influence Du Bois wielded, and concerned that they might give the appearance of "undue white influence" on NAACP policy, the board members sided with Du Bois. After all, they reasoned, to the emerging class of black urban professionals, Du Bois was the NAACP. To keep him affiliated with the organization, they granted him sweeping concessions to ensure that he had "free play to exercise all his abilities and energy and enthusiasm."

Unhappy with what he considered a lack of support from the board, Villard resigned as chairman. The NAACP's troubles remained, however, because the root cause of the problem was unresolved. Founded by liberal whites, the NAACP was established to reduce discrimination and poor treatment of blacks through lobbying and propaganda. More than half of the NAACP's annual budget of $11,000 was provided by 18 white philanthropists, who believed that the best way to fight racism was to de-emphasize it.

A continuing point of contention among black NAACP members like W. E. B. Du Bois was the white domination of the organization. A great deal of discussion ensued over whether white members should continue holding top-level positions in the organization. Du Bois in particular feared that white philanthropists favoring the causes of the NAACP would refuse to aid black-dominated organizations, thereby compromising the NAACP's integrationist program. White members such as Mary Ovington acknowledged such difficulties, but they believed that whites necessarily had to run the organization until blacks had sufficient political and economic resources to run the organization themselves.

Du Bois's radical words and actions alarmed white financial supporters, particularly when they began to believe that *The Crisis* was increasingly siding against whites. Even Ovington, Du Bois's most ardent supporter, grew concerned. In her autobiography, she admits that she wondered whether Du Bois had some need to offend white readers or make them uncomfortable by hurling epithets such as "reactionary heathens" at them. Had they been mistaken to believe that the NAACP could foster "work for colored and white people to do together," she wondered? Was the battle for racial equality meant for blacks to wage by themselves, without participation from whites?

On the opposite side of this dilemma was Du Bois and what he called the problem of the color line. He

Despite criticism of The Crisis, *W. E. B. Du Bois received support from Mary White Ovington, seen here in a photo with Arthur Spingarn on her right, one of the NAACP's first attorneys, and to her left John L. Lewis, president of the Congress of Industrial Organizations (C.I.O.). Her confidence in Du Bois probably helped him maintain his position as editor for 24 years.*

believed people like Villard could never fully understand that black people needed to build and run their own organizations and fight their own battles. Finally, at the November 1914 meeting of NAACP board members, the issue came to a head. They had tired of Du Bois's separatist agenda and believed that his presence was now detrimental to the smooth operation of the NAACP. They demanded that Du Bois be accountable to another board member, and they criticized him for spending too much time traveling around the country at the organization's expense, promoting himself and his newspaper but not the organization itself. Key officers complained that the time Du Bois spent on NAACP business was insufficient. Although the number of subscribers to *The Crisis* was growing exponentially, so were its operating costs. It was beginning to bleed the organization dry.

A proud man who refused to take orders from other board members, Du Bois attempted to make a clean break. He decided to relinquish his NAACP salary and assume full responsibility for *The Crisis*. He would accept only general guidance from a three-person committee appointed by the board with his concurrence. Not all of the board members turned their backs on Du Bois. Mary White Ovington continued to back him, explaining her position eloquently. "To me," she said, "the rest of us on the board are able journeymen doing one day's work to be forgotten tomorrow. But Du Bois is the master builder, whose work will speak to men as long as there is an oppressed race on the earth."

But even Ovington's undying support and good intentions did not fully resolve the bitter conflict between Du Bois and key NAACP board members. Du Bois had no interest in answering to the NAACP. He considered the struggle both personal and symbolic, saying, "Of course, the old thing that we always fear is tending to happen in the Association. It is becoming a white man's organization working for the colored people in which no colored people have any real power." In the white world, Du Bois claimed, ability, temperament, and determination were considered assets, but as his 50 years of experience had confirmed, "the colored man gets no such chance. He is seldom given authority or freedom; when he gets these things he gets them accidentally." He saw the same thing happening in the NAACP.

Du Bois was editor of *The Crisis* for 24 years before he retired in 1934. During that time the

Langston Hughes, an influential black author, often contributed articles to The Crisis. *The magazine often published the writings of some of the best-known figures in the civil rights community.*

newspaper boasted such influential contributors as playwright George Bernard Shaw, Indian nationalist leader Mahatma Gandhi, author Sinclair Lewis, writer Langston Hughes, and author and NAACP executive secretary James Weldon Johnson. Although *The Crisis* had been born as the official literary vehicle of the NAACP, it became virtually self-supporting, although at Du Bois's retirement its circulation had dropped to 10,000 from a peak of 100,000 in 1918. Roy Wilkins succeeded Du Bois and held the post until 1949, when James W. Ivy took over. Ivy was at the helm until 1967, the peak of the civil rights era. In 1988 the newspaper's circulation had risen to 350,000, and although *The Crisis* underwent a number of transitions in editorial philosophy, it is still in print today.

FOLLOW
the
PRESIDENT
OUTLAW
LYNCHING
N.A.A.C.P.
83
WOMEN
LYNCHED
SINCE 1889
N.A.A.C.P.
5,068
"CRIME"
SHOULD
CONSIDER

5

"Fearsome Reminders of Their Status": The Crusade Against Lynching

Members of the NAACP protest against lynching in Washington, D.C., December 11, 1934. Lynching, an act of vigilante "justice" in which a large group of people play judge, jury, and executioner, has been in existence since the Revolutionary War.

IN CAIRO, ILLINOIS, not long after the Springfield riots of August 1908, the murdered body of a white woman was found, and police in the town arrested and imprisoned a homeless black man named "Frog" James for the crime.

According to local newspaper accounts, after an angry white crowd formed around the police station where James was being held, thc sheriff and a deputy moved James by train out of town and into a wooded area, where the three remained overnight. But by morning the mob at the police station had grown, and eventually it left the station and headed for the woods where the prisoner had been hidden. The crowd found the sheriff and Frog James easily and returned James to town, dragging him by a noose around his neck into a prominent downtown area. There, they threw the other end of the rope around an overhanging light pole and hanged the man.

The newspapers reported that James was shot 500 times, and that some of the bullets severed the rope, causing his lifeless body to drop to the ground. In a gruesome parade, the man's corpse was then

A crowd of white men and women gather around the burning corpse of a lynching victim who had been tied to a tree and then burned alive. In the 1920s, 90 percent of the victims of lynching were black.

dragged once more through Cairo to the place where the white woman had been discovered. There, the mob publicly set fire to Frog James's body.

This kind of horrific lynching was justified by many whites, particularly in the South, as a "necessary response" to crimes perpetrated by blacks and to a legal system that they believed was ineffective. Offenses alleged to have been committed by victims of lynchings ranged from actual crimes such as murder, assault, theft, arson, and rape to trivial matters such as "disrespect" toward whites. A common example of this type of perceived disrespect was the failure to give way to whites on the sidewalk.

The most frequent justification for lynching was the accusation of rape or sexual assault of a white woman by a black man. Even though fewer than 26 percent of all lynchings actually involved this crime, the mythology of rape involved the images of black people—especially black men—as savage and monster-like, with a desire or need to attack or "despoil" white women. In this way, white southern males who engaged in such mob behavior rationalized their violent acts against African Americans.

Lynching mobs typically tried to elicit "confessions" from their victims. Often, they also allowed the victims to pray before their execution. It was not uncommon for the lynchers to leave the bullet-ridden bodies of hanging victims on public display as an ominous warning to other blacks to "stay in their places." Mob lynchings of blacks were often inconceivably brutal: they involved hangings, burnings, torture, mutilation, castration of male victims, and even dismemberment. A particularly ghastly aspect of lynchings was the taking of "souvenirs"—a grisly reminder of the event, such as a piece of the body, a bone fragment salvaged from the ashes, or a photograph of the lynching.

Although the practice of lynching—the taking of a person's life by mob violence—can be traced to the broad tradition of mob and small-group violence in America, the term is generally linked to the killing of African Americans by white mobs during the period between the end of the Civil War and the middle of the 20th century. The word "lynching" is commonly believed to date to a practice originated during the Revolutionary War, when a Colonel Charles Lynch and other prominent citizens of Bedford County, Virginia, informally gathered to apprehend and punish the lawless and the Tories (a group who supported British rule in America). Initially, lynch mobs punished alleged lawbreakers and enforced community values and beliefs through whippings, tarring and feathering, and occasional executions by hanging or shooting, even though the perpetrators themselves were never sanctioned by legal authorities. Most victims were white and ranged from outlaws and horse thieves in frontier areas to Catholics, immigrants, and abolitionists in Northern cities.

The lynching of blacks during the era of slavery was infrequent because it was not considered "economic" to kill laborers. Also, some slaves were viewed as extended family members, to be treated like children, and under a rigid system of control there was rarely a need for violence. In the aftermath of widespread slave rebellions, however, white mobs often sought out and violently punished suspected conspirators.

After the Civil War, lynchings became the symbol of southern white supremacy, as mobs resorted to violence to restore white control over former slaves. The crime reached its apex during the 1880s and 1890s, when more than 150 lynchings were recorded yearly. The *Chicago Tribune* began recording lynchings in 1882; from that year until 1968, the newspaper estimates that 4,742 people died at the hands of lynch mobs. Black men and women accounted for 72 percent of known lynchings after 1882. By the 1920s, 90 percent of victims were black, and 95 percent of all lynchings occurred in the South.

In the period following World War I, some areas of the United States resembled war zones, with whites attacking black neighborhoods and blacks counterattacking whenever possible. The deadliest of these disturbances occurred in July 1919 in Chicago, Illinois, where the drowning of a black boy sparked 13 days of rioting in which 38 people died and 537 were injured.

Most of the anti-black violence was spontaneous, but some of it was organized. The white supremacist Ku Klux Klan (KKK), founded after the Civil War in

Members of the Ku Klux Klan surround a line of men waiting to be inducted into the group's ranks. The KKK saw an increase in its membership and activities during the early 20th century.

an attempt to destroy black political power, had resurfaced in full force in the first decade of the 20th century, expanding its message of hate to include not only blacks, but also Jews, Catholics, immigrants, atheists, and anyone else deemed racially or morally "impure." White-robed Klan members viewed returning black war veterans as the most threatening group of all. Of the more than 70 blacks who were lynched in 1919, 10 were soldiers. Race riots and violence were so widespread and bloody that summer that it is often referred to as the Red Summer.

The NAACP aimed to combat such mob executions with a vast publicity campaign consisting of pamphlet dissemination, sponsorship of in-depth studies and discussions of the crimes, and numerous educational activities intended to mobilize public support for ending these atrocities. Its antilynching campaign was effective primarily because it strengthened the organization's branch structure, focusing on organizing new divisions across the country to carry out most of its protest activities.

For field secretary James Weldon Johnson, who organized the expansion, the most pressing task was to significantly increase the presence of the NAACP in the South, where most of the lynching was occurring. Although progress was initially slow, by the end of 1919 the NAACP had 310 branches, 31 of which were in southern states. The Atlanta branch, founded in 1916, was the region's strongest, with more than 1,000 members. From 1917 to 1919, the NAACP's total membership increased nearly tenfold, from 9,300 to 91,203.

One of the most famous figures in the crusade against lynching was Ida B. Wells-Barnett. In her autobiography, *Crusade for Justice*, the famous journalist and civil rights activist captures the grotesque absurdity of the practice. Wells-Barnett did as much to educate Americans about the horrors and misconceptions of lynchings as any other leader, black or white, during her lifetime, and was among the first to keep actual statistics on lynchings.

Ida B. Wells became an activist early in life. On May 4, 1884, the 22-year-old bought a first-class train ticket for her usual ride to work as a teacher in a rural Tennessee school. She had just taken her seat on the train, however, when the conductor told her that she would have to move to the smoking coach. He explained that, under the railroad's new "separate but equal" rules, blacks were restricted to the smoking car. Wells refused to move and fought two conductors who tried to remove her forcibly from her first-class seat. She got off the train instead, and she filed a lawsuit against the railroad for discrimination. Although she won in a local court, the state

Ida B. Wells-Barnett highlighted the grotesque acts of violence that took place during lynchings in her book Crusade for Justice. *Wells-Barnett used her influential stature as a newspaper publisher and journalist to shed light on the practices of lynching.*

supreme court reversed the decision in 1887. After the reversal, she expressed her outrage in a series of articles she wrote for a church newspaper. She described the railroad incident and encouraged her readers to join her and defy Jim Crow laws. She later lost her job as a teacher after writing several articles about the deplorable state of education for black children.

Eventually Wells-Barnett became part-owner of the *Memphis Star* newspaper. When three of her friends, all prominent black businessmen, were lynched on false charges in March 1892, she wrote searing editorials attacking Memphis's white public officials for "tolerating, encouraging, and participating" in the lynchings, and she encouraged her readers to move out of the area in protest. Within weeks of their publication, her newspaper office was ransacked and destroyed by a white mob.

Undaunted, Wells moved to New York, where she became a correspondent for several black newspapers and resumed her attack on black oppression and Jim Crow laws. The incident in Memphis had riveted her attention to the crime of lynching. White officials in the South, she declared, "insisted that lynching was a reluctantly imposed punishment required to protect white women from (free) black men, whom they mythologized as super-virile, lascivious, uncontrollably promiscuous, and bestial." She used her newspaper contacts to learn about lynchings as they occurred, and each time she heard of such an incident she traveled to the place where it occurred, often at her own expense and risking physical harm, to find and interview eyewitnesses.

Wells-Barnett's widely reported investigations substantiated the view that sexual assaults were indeed associated with lynchings—but she proved that the assaults usually took place at the hands of the lynchers, who often sexually humiliated and mutilated their victims. Wells-Barnett's thorough reporting substantiated her belief that "the offenses committed by lynching victims were likely to have been registering to vote, testifying in court against white people, not being deferential to white people, or simply being unfortunate enough to encounter a mob of whites on their way to another lynching." In one horrifyingly tragic example, a black Texan and his three sons were lynched for the "offense" of being the first in the county to harvest their cotton crop that season.

Wells-Barnett's reports dispelled the myth of lynchings as white justice and revealed them as mere terror tactics designed to be "fearsome reminders to black people of the status assigned to them and the apparent futility of any resistance to that assignment." In every major black newspaper, in pamphlets she wrote and distributed, and in passionate speeches to groups throughout the United States and England, she relayed her message. She was instrumental in forming several national and international human rights organizations that pressured the U.S. government to punish lynching and abolish the crime. More than any other individual, Ida Wells-Barnett was responsible for the worldwide condemnation of lynching that forced the federal government to take action and protect the lives of black people, especially in the South.

The NAACP's growing membership and geographic expansion helped greatly in the continuing battle against racial violence waged by activists like Ida Wells-Barnett. As the organization developed, blacks were taking key positions. Among them was James Weldon Johnson, named the first black NAACP secretary in 1921. But the NAACP's philosophy of agitation and education was proving ineffective against widespread race riots and lynchings, and its leaders ultimately decided to shift their focus to the political process.

Walter White, a young insurance salesman from Atlanta who joined the national staff in 1918 as an assistant secretary, was charged with investigating lynchings. A very light-skinned African American, White was effective in part because he could blend inconspicuously among whites. Soon after he joined the NAACP, the organization published a report

Walter White was able to use his light complexion, which enabled him to blend in with whites, to assist him in his investigations of lynchings.

entitled *Thirty Years of Lynching in the United States, 1889–1918*, which provided documentation that forced Congress to develop a plan for halting the widespread crime.

In 1920, a year after the report was published, the U.S. House of Representatives passed an antilynching bill, but Southern senators killed the bill in a filibuster (a tactic of delaying or preventing action in a legislative assembly). Although the bill failed to pass, the Republican Party continued its efforts to enact a similar law. The NAACP viewed this action as a strong indication that it was at last being taken seriously as a political force. Although no antilynching law ever passed in the U.S. Congress, the NAACP's campaign of public awareness helped to virtually do away with this act of racial violence.

6

The NAACP and the Courts

Thurgood Marshall (center) meets with fellow NAACP lawyers in Pittsburgh, Pennsylvania. Marshall was one of a growing number of young attorneys who supported the NAACP's attempts to counter racial inequality with legal arguments.

IN THE EARLY 1950s, the Reverend Oliver Brown sued the board of education of Topeka, Kansas, on behalf of Linda Brown, his elementary-school-age daughter. Brown was challenging the legality of a Kansas law that permitted "separate but equal" school facilities for black and white students. Because the neighborhood school just seven blocks from the Browns' home was for whites only, the girl was forced to walk to a bus stop six blocks away across a dangerous railroad yard, ride a bus for an hour and 20 minutes, and then wait a half hour before the blacks-only school 20 blocks from her home opened for the day.

The case, called *Brown v. Board of Education of Topeka*, ultimately reached the U.S. Supreme Court as part of a larger case in 1954. A companion case being considered at the same time involved segregation in South Carolina's public schools, as required by the state constitution. In statistics from Clarendon County, South Carolina, where the case was brought to court, it was not difficult to see the inequity of the separate but equal laws. In 1949 and 1950, the average expenditure for white students was $179; for blacks it was $43. The county's 2,375 white students attended schools with superior facilities in buildings worth a total of $673,850. The same county's 6,531 black students attended school in buildings valued at $194,575; many of these facilities lacked even basic necessities such as indoor plumbing and heating. Teachers in the black schools received, on average, salaries that were one-third less than those of teachers in the white schools. Clarendon County provided school buses for white students, but it refused to provide transportation for blacks.

The NAACP's involvement in bringing the *Brown v. Board of Education of Topeka* case to the federal courts demonstrated its growing political power. With its own lawyers, the NAACP had handled hundreds of civil rights cases even before it began its thrust for political influence. In the NAACP's early legal campaigns, there were very few good black lawyers, so the organization relied mainly on the pro bono services of white lawyers, including Arthur Spingarn, his law partner Charles H. Studin, and Moorfield Storey. Arthur Spingarn assumed leadership of the NAACP's legal committee in 1929.

The NAACP's first significant court case was an attempt to save the life of an illiterate farmhand in South Carolina. "Pink" Franklin had been sentenced to death for killing a police officer who attempted to arrest him. Franklin had tried to leave his employer after he had received advances on his wages. The case is noteworthy because it forced the U.S. Supreme Court to address the issue of citizenship rights for African Americans. Although the court upheld the guilty ruling, the NAACP did convince South Carolina's governor to commute (change) Franklin's sentence to life imprisonment rather than death.

The NAACP's first legal victory came in 1915 when its lawyers won the *Guinn v. United States* case, in which they had challenged the constitutionality of Oklahoma's "grandfather clause"—a provision stipulating that prospective voters had to pass a test or pay

Much of the NAACP's early legal representation came from lawyers, such as Arthur Spingarn (left), seen here with Roy Wilkins, who performed their services for free.

a tax unless they were descendants of men who had voted before 1867. The U.S. Supreme Court ruled that the clause violated the Fifteenth Amendment, which gave black men the right to vote. The victory motivated the NAACP to continue to seek out important court cases and educate both whites and blacks about racial wrongs in American education and political life.

To members of the NAACP, the task of educating white Americans was an even greater challenge than resolving specific problems concerning race. Thus, the NAACP had two criteria for accepting a court case: First, it had to involve discrimination and injustice based on race or color; and second, it had to establish a precedent (serve as an example for similar future cases) for protecting the rights of African Americans as a group. As the NAACP continued its legal assault on segregation, it sought to end its dependence on volunteer lawyers as well—a practice that had proved a major handicap in the *Powell v. Alabama* case that began in 1931. That year in Scottsboro, Alabama, nine African Americans, two of them boys aged 13 and 14, were charged with raping two white girls on a freight train in which they had all been riding. Eight of the nine were found guilty and sentenced to death. The Supreme Court of Alabama set aside one of the convictions.

The U.S. Supreme Court did not permit the convictions to stand, however, because the men were young, uneducated, and given inadequate access to legal counsel. "[F]aced with public hostility and in a fight for their lives," it said, the men "required the best and most competent lawyers available. Instead, they had been given only token legal representation." The Supreme Court decided that in capital cases where the accused was unable to obtain his own counsel and was not skilled enough to defend himself, it was up to the trial court to assume the responsibility of assigning appropriate legal representation. Failure to do so, it said, was a violation of due process of law.

Four years after what was commonly called the Scottsboro case, the NAACP established the Legal Defense and Educational Fund, the primary aim of which was to boldly challenge the constitutionality of "separate but equal" laws, especially if and when they were accompanied by discrimination. The NAACP decided to focus on the glaring disparities between white and black schools.

As its first special counsel, the NAACP hired Charles H. Houston, the highly respected dean of the Howard University School of Law. Houston brought a new strategy to the legal department. He intended

The NAACP New York City headquarters during the mid-1930s. It was around this time that the NAACP first launched its campaign to legally end segregation in U.S. schools.

to force state governments either to strengthen black institutions or to abandon them because of the expense of maintaining separate facilities. To accumulate evidence of unequal funding, Houston and his protégé, Thurgood Marshall, toured the South to investigate academic conditions.

Houston's first line of attack was graduate and professional schools. He successfully tested this strategy in the 1935 Maryland Supreme Court case *Murray v. Maryland*, the first in a series of challenges that would lead to the *Brown* case. Houston was succeeded as NAACP special counsel in 1938 by Marshall, a Howard University Law School graduate who vigorously continued the attack begun by his predecessor.

Between 1950 and 1952, the lawyers for the Legal Defense and Educational Fund brought strong suits against school segregation not only in South Carolina and Kansas, but also in Virginia, Delaware, and Washington, D.C. At the time, 17 states and the District of Columbia permitted legal school segregation and several other states allowed school districts to maintain separate schools at their discretion. In theory, these schools were supposed to be equal in quality, but in reality this was never the case. As local courts ruled against plaintiffs, the Legal Defense and Educational Fund submitted the cases to the U.S. Supreme Court for appeal. Finally, the Court consolidated the five cases and gave them a single hearing on December 9, 1952. This enormous NAACP case against school segregation was given the title *Brown v. Board of Education of Topeka*, after the much smaller Kansas suit of the same name.

On May 17, 1954, the Supreme Court handed down its landmark ruling on the case. Chief Justice Earl Warren read the Court's unanimous decision before a rapt audience:

> Does segregation of children in public schools solely on the basis of race, even though the physical facilities and other "tangible" factors may be equal, deprive the children of the minority group of equal education opportunities? We believe that it does. . . . We conclude that in the field of public education, the doctrine of "separate but equal" has no place.

Brown v. Board of Education of Topeka was the most important legal case affecting African Americans in the 20th century, and is one of the most significant Supreme Court decisions in U.S. history. The case grew in symbolism to become an inspiration for the civil rights movement, and eventually led to the elimination of all laws of segregation in the United States.

Thurgood Marshall's bold legal challenge to segregation also led the U.S. Supreme Court to reconsider older cases, particularly *Plessy v. Ferguson*, the 1896 ruling that established the separate but equal doctrine in the first place. The Supreme Court was also compelled to examine the true meaning of the Fourteenth Amendment, which had been composed during a period when most states allowed at least

In delivering the Supreme Court's decision in Brown v. Board of Education of Topeka, *Chief Justice Earl Warren said "the doctrine of 'separate but equal' has no place" in the United States.*

some forms of segregation and when public education in the South was largely undeveloped.

Although the *Brown* decision was a great victory for the NAACP, African Americans, and the United States in general, it did not bring an immediate end to segregated schools. Instead, the Supreme Court ordered new arguments to be heard the following year that would help it determine the best way to begin the difficult process of desegregation. In a second case commonly known as *Brown II* (1955), the Supreme Court ordered its original ruling implemented with "all deliberate speed," although in practice the process was extremely slow. For example, Linda Brown, the plaintiff in the original *Brown* case, did not attend integrated schools until she was a teen, and none of the juvenile plaintiffs in the Clarendon County case ever attended integrated schools.

The executive director of the NAACP, Roy Wilkins, accompanied by civil rights advocate Attorney General Robert Kennedy, during an NAACP march on the Justice Building in Washington D.C., June, 1964. During the 1950s Wilkins played a major role in ensuring that states complied with the Brown *decision.*

The course involved in implementing the *Brown* decision was long and complex, and it was hindered by lingering attitudes of racial discrimination, especially among whites who were unwilling to change the status quo. The NAACP refused to be satisfied with the mere decision to end segregation, however; it intended to force the execution of the federal ruling at all costs.

Under executive director Roy Wilkins, NAACP lawyers participated in shaping desegregation plans, and they monitored compliance with *Brown* across the country. In 1956, for example, with NAACP sponsorship, Autherine Lucy, an African-American woman, won a court ruling allowing her to enroll at the University of Alabama. University officials then expelled her on the pretext of preventing racial violence. After the court ordered Lucy's readmission to the university, she was expelled a second time by the school's board of trustees. The incident quickly made it clear that many southern institutions were not

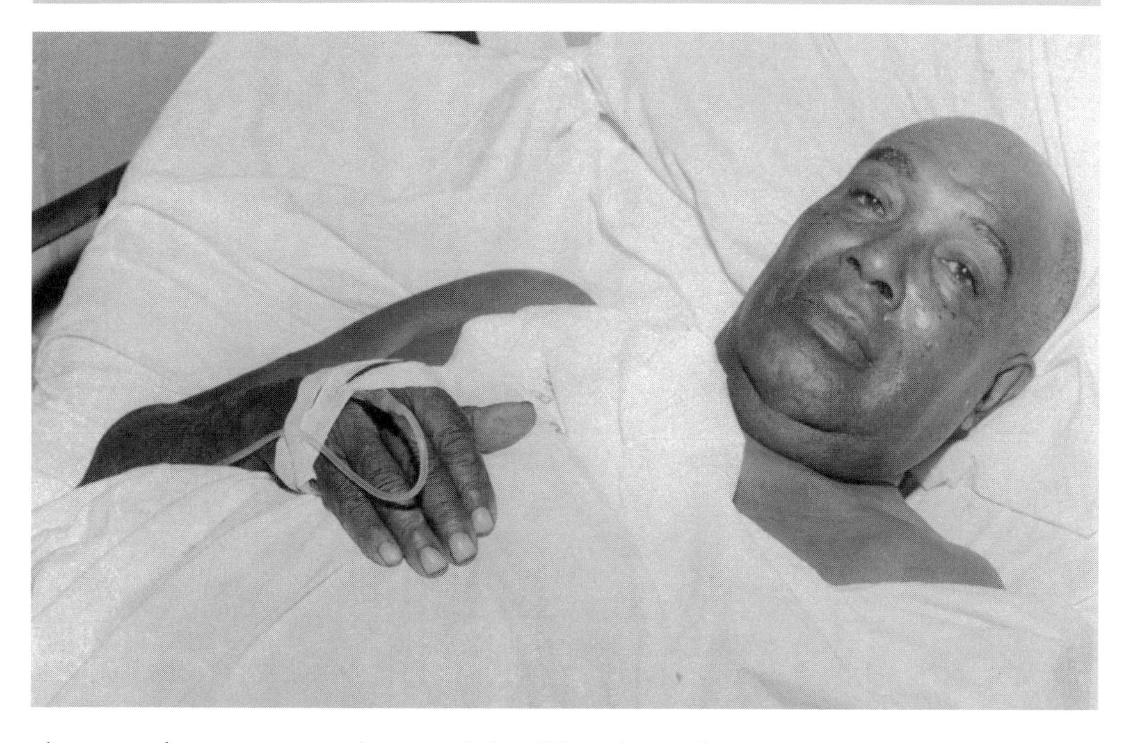

Gus Courts lies in a hospital bed after being wounded during a shooting in Belzoni, Mississippi, that resulted in the death of two of his fellow NAACP officials. The Brown *decision and its implementation, particularly in the South, often was met with violent resistance.*

about to desegregate without a fight. The NAACP poured its time and financial resources into the battle, and its trailblazing victories in the courts, especially the *Brown* decision, made it a main target of the South's campaign of "massive resistance."

The campaign against integration once more revived the activities of the Ku Klux Klan, which played a major role in the backlash of racial violence in the South. The KKK was only one of many organized threats that the NAACP faced, however. Just as Ida Wells-Barnett had learned 30 years earlier, when some southern whites perceived a threat to their way of life, they retaliated with force. Less than two months after the *Brown* decision was handed down, southern political leaders, businessmen, and other members of the professional elite organized the White Citizens' Council in Mississippi. Some called the council "manicured kluxism." Almost immediately, similar "councils" arose in other states, using economic and political pressure to prevent implementation of the *Brown* ruling. In March 1956, nearly all of the southerners in Congress defied *Brown* by signing a "Southern Manifesto" that declared the Court decision "illegal."

Before the *Brown* decision, white racists had traditionally targeted blacks individually, attempting to intimidate and control them with lynchings and other acts of terror and violence. In the 1950s, Southern whites began using such tactics not only as a means to terrorize individuals but also in an attempt to disrupt entire organizations—including the NAACP. For example, on Christmas night in 1951, the Mims, Florida, home of NAACP field secretary Harry T. Moore was bombed. Moore died in the blast; his wife died a few days later from injuries sustained in the explosion. In 1955, the Reverend George W. Lee and Lamar Smith, NAACP officials in Belzoni, Mississippi, were shot to death; Gus Courts, president of the Belzoni NAACP branch, was wounded in the shooting and was later forced to abandon his store and flee to Chicago.

The NAACP charged that these acts of violence were direct retaliations against those who fostered the recent civil rights decisions. It demanded that the U.S. Department of Justice protect blacks in Mississippi and anywhere else in the South where whites were terrorizing blacks. The Justice Department responded by declaring its lack of authority to prosecute suspected murderers and civil rights violators in what it claimed were state jurisdictions.

In December 1955, the NAACP board of directors voted to deposit $20,000 in the Tri-State Bank in Memphis, Tennessee, to increase the bank's reserves and enable it to make more loans to local blacks. The board also called for an investigation of the federal "surplus commodities" program in Mississippi, which provided food to the destitute, to see whether it was discriminating against blacks. The NAACP pushed for a meeting with the Mississippi Power and Light Com-

President Eisenhower is seen here meeting with civil rights leaders, including Martin Luther King Jr., just to the president's right, and Roy Wilkins, seen standing at the far right of the photograph. Eisenhower supported civil rights legislation but was opposed to providing federal enforcement of the law.

pany to challenge the company's practice of cutting off power to businessmen affiliated with the NAACP and then overcharging them to have service restored.

Despite violence and threats against members and sympathizers, the NAACP continued to grow. During 1955, the number of NAACP chapters in Mississippi more than doubled, from 10 to 21, and membership in that state increased by 100 percent. In 1956, Louisiana led the South in a more deliberate assault on the NAACP when the state attorney general demanded that the organization's local chapters file their membership lists with the state. When the NAACP refused, the attorney general obtained an injunction barring the organization from operating in Louisiana. The states of Alabama, Texas, and Georgia followed with similar legal actions.

In 1958, the U.S. Supreme Court overturned Alabama's fine of $100,000 against the NAACP, levied because the organization had refused to disclose the names and addresses of its members. However, the Court did not lift the injunction that barred the NAACP from operating in Alabama. Furthermore, the Arkansas and Florida supreme courts held that the U.S. Supreme Court's ruling did not affect their states. Not until June 1, 1964, after four appeals, did the U.S. Supreme Court unanimously rule that the NAACP had a legal right to register in Alabama as a foreign corporation. The ruling in effect overturned similar bans against the NAACP in other Southern states; it also paved the way for the NAACP to resume normal operations in Alabama four months later.

The South's intensely negative response to the Supreme Court rulings against segregation prompted the NAACP to passionately renew its call for enforcing the *Brown* decision. It appealed to President Dwight D. Eisenhower, pointing out that his leadership was essential to defeat steadfast southern resistance to the passage of civil rights laws by Congress. Although Eisenhower was a state's rights advocate, in the end he supported the NAACP's demand that discrimination in federally funded programs and in the armed forces was unacceptable. Still, Eisenhower was opposed to taking federal action to enforce the *Brown* decision.

Civil rights proponents were essentially left with what became a weak voting rights law. The Civil Rights Act passed on September 9, 1957, created a division of civil rights in the Justice Department and a bipartisan Civil Rights Commission. In retrospect, however, the Civil Rights Act is seen as extremely influential because it was not only the first such bill passed by Congress in 82 years, but it also broke the psychological barriers to civil rights, making it easier for future legislative efforts to succeed.

This encouraging breakthrough was somewhat overshadowed by another significant event that

occurred in September 1957, in Little Rock, Arkansas. There, Governor Orval Faubus called up the Arkansas National Guard to block implementation of a federal court desegregation order at Central High School. To uphold the U.S. Constitution and end rioting, President Eisenhower federalized the Arkansas National Guard troops and ordered 1,000 members of the 101st Airborne Division (of the regular armed services) into Little Rock. His action enabled nine black students to attend the school. Federalized troops escorted the youngsters, known as the "Little Rock Nine," into the high school building. It was the first time since the Civil War that a U.S. president had dispatched American troops to the South to protect the constitutional rights of African Americans—and it was a major turning point in the struggle for racial equality in the South.

The National Guard line the streets of Little Rock, Arkansas, in order to enforce the desegregation of a local high school. The protection provided by the National Guard allowed nine black students to attend the high school and proved to be a major victory for the civil rights movement.

7

Marching Toward Freedom

Martin Luther King Jr. leads a protest march in Montgomery, Alabama, following the arrest of Rosa Parks for refusing to give up her seat on a public city bus.

ON DECEMBER 1, 1955, a black woman named Rosa Parks was arrested for violating the Montgomery, Alabama, segregation law after she refused to surrender her bus seat to a white passenger. Angered by the arrest, black activists formed the Montgomery Improvement Association to boycott the city transit system and named Dr. Martin Luther King Jr., a young, well-educated newcomer to the city, as its president.

In King's first address to Montgomery Improvement Association members, he made it clear that he believed they had no alternative but to organize a protest against Parks's arrest. He admitted that African Americans had, up to that point, shown admirable patience in the national fight for freedom and equality. Now, he continued, he had begun to suspect that many whites believed that blacks actually liked such second-class treatment. King assured association members that they were about to exercise a new kind of patience now—patience for nothing less than freedom and justice.

With his address, King launched a new era in the struggle for racial equality. He provided a fresh voice and a new way for blacks to view themselves as citizens. King's expert and inspired rhetoric quickly drew many followers, both black and white, and though his own home was bombed and his family's safety threatened, he continued with the bus boycott. Finally, on December 20, 1956, the U.S. Supreme Court upheld a lower court's decision declaring Montgomery's segregated bus seating unconstitutional. After a 381-day boycott, Montgomery was forced to desegregate its public buses.

The NAACP had inspired the boycott in part with its legal victories against segregation. Many organizers of the boycott were local NAACP leaders as well, but the nonviolent demonstration technique that the boycott adopted was a substantial departure from the NAACP's well-defined legal and political program for civil rights. Believers in this new strategy, which involved not only boycotts but also sit-ins and direct nonviolent confrontation, began to forge a rift among NAACP members.

In 1959, the NAACP celebrated the 50th anniversary of its founding. With membership near 400,000, the organization began some of the most challenging activism in its history. That year, the NAACP chapter at Washington University in St. Louis, Missouri, conducted sit-ins to end segregation at local lunch counters. The NAACP Youth Council organized several such demonstrations, but its activities failed to capture national media attention because they were not conducted in the Deep South, where the most virulent opposition to black civil rights flourished. On February 1, 1960, however, when four students from North Carolina Agricultural and Technical College staged a similar sit-in at a segregated Woolworth's lunch counter in Greensboro, the demonstration attracted massive media attention. African Americans made up more than 20 percent of Woolworth's business, yet the company would not let blacks eat at its lunch counters and refused to treat black shoppers the same way as its white customers.

Protesters Joseph McNeil (left) and Franklin McCain (second from left) reenact the 1960 sit-in demonstration at a lunch counter in Greensboro, North Carolina. With them are Clarence Henderson (far right) and Billy Smith, who participated in later lunch counter demonstrations.

Although another group, the Congress of Racial Equality (CORE), had also held sit-ins as early as the 1940s, the 1960 Greensboro protest earned more attention than any previous demonstration. The growing popularity of television was one of the reasons for this phenomenon, and the success of the Montgomery bus boycott piqued the press and general public's interest in the story of the civil rights struggle.

The four college students who sat at the Greensboro lunch counter—Franklin McCain, Ezell Blair Jr., Joseph McNeil, and David Richmond—made history as they sat quietly from 2:00 P.M. until closing. They studied as they waited, and refused to leave until they were served. They returned the following day and sat down at the counter again, even though they were told it was "closed." Twenty-three other students joined them.

The quiet protest became a media event, and the NAACP was heavily involved in the sit-in. George Simpkins and Ralph Jones, officials of the Greensboro branch of the NAACP, worked closely with the protesters as consultants. Word spread quickly, and soon thousands of students, mostly blacks but also a few whites, began staging similar protests at lunch counters and in other public places across the South. In the next 18 months, thousands of students participated in sit-ins to protest the unjust treatment of African Americans; more than 3,600 of them were arrested and jailed.

The protesters were trained to be nonviolent and to protect themselves. They were careful not to carry any sharp objects (pens, pencils, keys, toothpicks) so that they could not be charged with violence. They used extreme measures to prepare themselves, including listening to racial slurs and having cigarettes crushed in their hair. They learned how to make their bodies limp and how to curl themselves into balls to protect their stomachs and internal organs. Brave and disciplined, these young men and women broke down the wall of segregation in public facilities in the United States. Even before the passage of the 1964 Civil Rights Act, which legislated an end to racial discrimination and segregation, hundreds of small southern communities and large cities were forced to desegregate lunch counters and other public venues. Nashville, Tennessee, was the first southern town to do so; Greensboro relented on July 25, 1960.

A great number of the younger NAACP members in the South were participating in the sit-ins. Branch officials, particularly Mississippi field secretary Medgar Evers, were responsible for coordinating many of the protest campaigns. Despite such involvement in the civil rights struggle, some younger members of the NAACP had become impatient with the organization's slow pace and passive resistance methods. They questioned whether the NAACP's carefully executed legal and political programs were still effective in such confrontational times.

The differing philosophies sparked a dramatic clash of strategies; the NAACP officially continued to adhere to its philosophy of change through court action and legislation, while Dr. King and the students of the Youth Council marched under the banner of nonviolent direct action and grass-roots change. The clash took tangible shape in 1959, when executive director Roy Wilkins suspended Robert Williams, president of the Monroe, North Carolina, branch for insisting that the NAACP meet "violence with violence."

Medgar Evers, a field secretary in Mississippi, helped to organize young protesters for a highly effective campaign of civil disobedience against continuing segregation in the South.

Despite the ideological rift and intense competition for financial contributions, media attention, and historical recognition, the young activists' strategy actually complemented that of the national NAACP. Ultimately the organization allocated large sums of money to bail out jailed demonstrators and provide them with legal support. It even joined more militant groups in local alliances, such as the Council of Federated Organizations (COFO), which sponsored voter registration and other activities in Mississippi.

By 1962, the NAACP had more than 388,000 members in 46 states and the District of Columbia. Its growth was remarkable, considering the flurry of repeated court injunctions, state administrative regulations, punitive legislation, and other intimidating actions that prevented many southerners from joining the NAACP. Moreover, these barriers created opportunities for other groups to establish themselves. Among these were the Southern Christian Leadership Conference (SCLC), organized in Atlanta, Georgia, in 1957 by King and his followers,

Stokely Carmichael led the efforts of the Student Nonviolent Coordinating Committee and was a vocal critic of the NAACP. He held that African Americans could make greater strides through more forceful and direct action against oppression.

and the Student Nonviolent Coordinating Committee (SNCC), organized with the aid of NAACP veteran Ella Baker, an inspiring African-American political activist who attracted many young members by getting them involved in the sit-in movement.

The goal of the SCLC was to coordinate and assist local organizations working for the full equality of African Americans in every aspect of daily life. Working primarily in the South, King and the SCLC conducted leadership-training programs, citizen-education projects, and voter-registration drives. The conference also played a major role in coordinating the civil rights march on Washington, D.C., in 1963 and in antidiscrimination and voter-registration drives, notably in Albany, Georgia, and Birmingham and Selma, Alabama, in the early 1960s. These campaigns in turn spurred passage of the federal Civil Rights Act of 1964 and the Voting Rights Act of 1965.

The Civil Rights Act of 1964 was created by legislators in an attempt to end discrimination based on race, color, religion, or national origin. This act is widely considered the most important piece of U.S. legislation on civil rights since Reconstruction. The act guarantees equal voting rights for all citizens and prohibits segregation or discrimination in public places. The Voting Rights Act of 1965 provides for the assignment of federal examiners to conduct registration and observe voting in states or counties where patterns of discrimination exist.

The Student Nonviolent Coordinating Committee, founded in 1960 in Raleigh, North Carolina, originally consisted of black and white college students who launched peaceful protests as a means to speed up desegregation in the South. In 1964, for instance, the SNCC sponsored the Mississippi Project, in which about 800 volunteers helped thousands of African Americans register to vote.

In 1966, however, the SNCC gained a new leader, Stokely Carmichael, who expressed the frustration and impatience of many young blacks over the slow success of nonviolent protest. He called for a campaign to fight the "white power" that had oppressed blacks with "black power," urging African Americans to seize political and economic control of their own communities. He rejected white support for the SNCC. The SNCC's new official stance was in stark contrast with that of the NAACP.

Probably best known for its legal and lobbying contributions to the civil rights movement, the NAACP had diligently monitored the gradual implementation of civil rights initiatives. In 1958, the organization forced the University of Florida to desegregate, and a similar lawsuit was pending with the University of Georgia when it desegregated in 1961. The following year, the NAACP headed the battle to desegregate the University of Mississippi, and after it was ordered to do so, Governor Ross

Martin Luther King Jr. delivers his famous "I Have a Dream" speech on August 28, 1963. King, one of the most dynamic figures of the civil rights movement, proved that large-scale peaceful protest could force change.

Barnett defied the federal court order and impelled President John F. Kennedy to send federal troops to the school to assure that James H. Meredith, the black student seeking admission, would be permitted to attend.

The NAACP was also instrumental in convincing Congress to pass the 1960 Civil Rights Act, but it was seen as merely a watered-down voting rights amendment to the 1957 act. President Kennedy had refused to send any bill to Congress because he believed that the legislative body would not pass comprehensive civil rights legislation. In February of 1963, however, he submitted a weak civil rights bill. The NAACP immediately powered an aggressive campaign to strengthen and support the bill.

Led by Dr. King, demonstrations in Birmingham, Alabama, provoked a national outrage and helped reshape the civil rights bill and strengthen the NAACP's drive to fortify it. On June 11, in response to the demonstrations, President Kennedy delivered a televised address on civil rights. The next night, Mississippi NAACP field secretary Medgar Evers was assassinated in Jackson. On June 19, the day Evers was buried, Kennedy sent Congress a revised and much more powerful civil rights bill.

One of the most important events of the civil rights movement was the March on Washington for Jobs and Freedom, held in 1963. A. Philip Randolph, a prominent voice in demanding the desegregation of federal offices and one of the founders of the AFL-CIO, called for the march, and the NAACP, along with Martin Luther King Jr. and other civil rights leaders, organized it. The NAACP took pains to ensure that the march's focus was broad enough to include the legislative battle for civil rights.

The NAACP made an effort to draw together multiple forces for peaceful change and to show the nation—and the world—the importance of solving America's racial unrest. Still, a few key black figures were not invited to participate because of their radical or anti-integrationist beliefs. Most notable among them was Nation of Islam national minister and spokesman Malcolm X, and the Nation's leader, Elijah Muhammad.

More than 200,000 people of all races attended the march on August 28, 1963. Among the many inspiring speakers was Dr. King, who electrified the crowd with his now-famous "I Have a Dream" address. The event powerfully demonstrated that people could gather peaceably, as they did in the shadow of the Lincoln Memorial, and demand justice and equality for all Americans.

Three months later, President John F. Kennedy was assassinated. His successor, Lyndon B. Johnson, vowed to see the slain president's civil rights bill through Congress, and he provided the forceful leadership that the NAACP had demanded from the executive office. The Civil Rights Act of 1964 was an immense victory for the NAACP. It enforced the constitutional right to vote and guaranteed relief

Lyndon B. Johnson shakes the hand of Martin Luther King Jr. following the signing of the 1964 Civil Rights Act.

against discrimination in public facilities. Among its provisions, it also granted authority to the U.S. attorney general to institute lawsuits to protect the constitutional rights of African Americans in public accommodations and public education, to extend the Commission on Civil Rights, to prohibit discrimination in federally assisted programs, and to establish a Commission on Equal Employment Opportunity.

The NAACP did not rest with the passage of the Civil Rights Act, however. Instead, it began working on protecting black voters' rights. Dr. King launched another peaceful march from Selma to Montgomery, Alabama, to protest what he called "continuing disfranchisement," the act of depriving black citizens of their rights of citizenship. The NAACP's successes had softened the national climate and created a positive atmosphere for the protest. As in the *Brown* decision, the NAACP was also particularly interested in public school desegregation, employment, and housing issues.

Despite the enormous changes wrought by the NAACP, its efforts were still not enough for some. In the new era of civil rights, an increasing number of young African Americans scorned the interracial structure and integrationist philosophy of the NAACP. These urban activists viewed the organization as old-fashioned and overly cautious. The cycle of urban racial violence during the 1960s in some ways indicated that the NAACP's programs were no longer appealing to the majority of frustrated urban youths.

The NAACP continued its strategy of legal recourse despite the intense criticism from younger activists. Fearful of a struggle over the passage of fair housing legislation, many black leaders sought a compromise and asked President Johnson to issue a comprehensive executive order that would bar discrimination in government-sponsored housing programs and federally insured mortgages. Johnson eventually agreed to sign the 1968 Fair Housing Act, but the act was not as strong as the NAACP had hoped. On one of the final days of the battle to pass the Fair Housing Act, Martin Luther King Jr. was assassinated in Memphis, Tennessee. The day after his death, civil rights leaders met at the White House to urge Congress to pass the bill as a tribute to Dr. King.

8

Past Victories and Future Challenges

Benjamin Chavis addresses the congregation of a black church in New York City shortly before being removed from his position with the NAACP. Chavis's tenure as NAACP director was plagued with controversy.

AFTER THE TURBULENCE of the 1960s subsided, the NAACP faced new challenges that were decidedly different from any it had previously encountered. "New" forms of racism were more systematic and indirect, more difficult to identify, and the NAACP needed fresh strategies to combat them.

One approach that appeared effective was the development of affirmative action and minority hiring programs with government and private businesses. The NAACP also began concerning itself with the administration of the death penalty in the American legal system. Its Legal Defense and Educational Fund monitored death penalty cases and compiled statistics that showed that African Americans were sentenced to die at a far higher rate than were whites. Three cases were brought to the Supreme Court concerning the death penalty and the racial biases present in the selection process. In all three cases, juries had convicted and imposed the death penalty on the accused without any concrete legal guidelines. As a result, in June 1972 in the case of *Furman v. Georgia*, the U.S. Supreme Court held that the death penalty constituted cruel and unusual punishment, which violated the Eighth Amendment. It was the first time the Supreme Court had ever ruled against the death penalty. The actual decision, however, created three options for use of the death penalty: mandatory death sentences for certain crimes, the development of standardized guidelines for juries, and the outright abolition of the penalty. In a later ruling, *Gregg v. Georgia,* the Court favored the creation of guidelines for juries.

The NAACP has also worked to prevent Supreme Court nominees with poor voting records on civil rights issues from being appointed. In 1969 the NAACP scored a double victory against two such nominees, one from South Carolina and another from Florida.

From its founding, the NAACP has also focused on abolishing media stereotypes, monitoring print media and later television and radio in an attempt to ensure that minorities are fairly portrayed. Although still in its infancy in 1915, the NAACP quickly launched a 10-year campaign of protest against D. W. Griffith's newly released film *Birth of a Nation,* which featured racist portrayals of African Americans. The NAACP charged that the film "assassinated" the character of African Americans and undermined the very basis of the black struggle for racial equality. The association also organized picketing of movie theaters and lobbied local governments to ban showings of the film.

In the early 1950s, NAACP pressure succeeded in removing *Amos 'n' Andy*—a radio program that later became a TV series—from network first-run television. The program featured derogatory stereotypes of two black characters who were played by white actors. In the 1960s the NAACP was partly responsible for creating and launching the television series *Julia,* the first to feature a positively portrayed African American in the lead role. In 1985, the NAACP organized protests of Steven Spielberg's film

A poster for the 1915 motion picture The Birth of a Nation, *which depicted Klansmen as heroes. The NAACP led a 10-year protest following the release of the controversial film.*

The Color Purple, based on Alice Walker's novel of the same name. The organization expressed concern over the idea of a white director telling a black story and portraying black situations and characters.

Other obstacles and challenges would also mold the NAACP into a modern organization, including financial problems and frequent changes in administration. The organization also faced continued criticism from blacks who believed it had fallen out of step with the needs of present-day African Americans. One of the lowest points for the NAACP came in 1977, at the end of Roy Wilkins's tenure as director. In 1976 a Mississippi court had awarded state highway patrolman Robert Moody $250,000 in a lawsuit he had filed against the NAACP. Moody charged that he had been libeled and slandered by the organization, whose local officials and state field director charged him with police brutality for allegedly beating a black man during a drunk-driving arrest. The NAACP had to borrow money to post the required $262,000 bond, although it eventually won a reversal of the judgment in an appeal. Following this case, a Hinds County court in Jackson, Mississippi, handed down another judgment against the NAACP as a result of a local lawsuit filed against it by Jackson businessmen after NAACP members boycotted their stores. Under Mississippi law, the NAACP was required to post a cash bond amounting to 125 percent of the judgment, which exceeded $1.5 million, or have its assets seized pending an appeal.

In addition to financial woes, the NAACP also experienced some setbacks related to the 1964 Civil Rights Act. In 1978, in the *Regents of the University of California v. Bakke* case, the Supreme Court ruled 5–4 that according to Title VI of the Civil Rights Act, which sought to prevent discrimination in any program that receives federal funds, the university's medical school could not maintain a special admissions program for African Americans. The Court ordered that the university medical school admit a white applicant, who had been rejected because of his race. The Court would later rule that race was a constitutionally valid criterion for admissions programs, and it also tightened the constitutional tests that minority groups needed to pass to develop specific civil rights programs.

The election of conservative Republican Ronald Reagan as president in 1980 effectively weakened the Civil Rights Commission, the Civil Rights Division of the Justice Department, and the Equal Employment Commission. In 1984, Benjamin Hooks led a 125,000-person March on Washington to protest what he called the "legal lynching" of civil rights by

Benjamin Hooks served as director of the NAACP from 1977 to 1993. Although he faced some opposition from other members of the NAACP's board, Hooks was an accomplished leader during his tenure.

the Reagan administration. Under Reagan, the NAACP had even greater difficulties developing effective new programs to meet the demands of post-civil rights America.

Benjamin Hooks, who in 1977 succeeded Roy Wilkins as director of the NAACP, accomplished many things during his tenure, which lasted until 1993. However, many people who were concerned about the survival of the organization questioned his ability to lead, until in 1983 the board chair, Margaret

Wilson, suspended him. Outraged that Wilson suspended the executive director without its approval, the board in turn fired her and reinstated Hooks. The upheaval was followed by a series of internal battles over the next three years, during which three successive people served as board chair. Despite internal chaos, Hooks secured promising financial agreements from several corporations, including $1 billion from the American Gas Association, earmarked for providing jobs and other economic opportunities for blacks under a fair-share program.

When Hooks retired in April 1993, the board of directors cast about for his replacement. Prominent political leader Jessie Jackson was among several likely candidates, but in the end, the board selected the Reverend Benjamin F. Chavis Jr. A radical departure from Hooks, Chavis had spent more than four years in prison after being falsely accused and convicted in 1972 on charges of conspiracy to commit arson, for setting fire to a grocery store in Wilmington, North Carolina. One reason Chavis was chosen over other candidates was his youth. Much younger than Hooks and the other candidates under consideration, Chavis seemed to be the right candidate to appeal to younger African Americans. The board hoped that he would revitalize the NAACP by attracting new sources of funding and reaching out to young African Americans.

Chavis's tenure with the NAACP was controversial and short, however. In fulfilling his promise of attracting young blacks, he began steering the organization in a militant direction. Chavis did succeed in drawing younger members into the NAACP, and he was praised for his courage in meeting with gang leaders to find ways to prevent street violence. Still, he shifted NAACP policy and embraced black separatist groups, such as the Nation of Islam, whose actions and philosophy the NAACP had consistently denounced. He was widely criticized for inviting leaders such as Nation of Islam head Louis Farrakhan to a black leadership conference, and for refusing to disassociate himself from the Nation's anti-Semitic declarations. As a result, NAACP membership dropped significantly.

Members also criticized Chavis's administrative policies and his unauthorized statements, such as his sanctioning (without consulting board members) of the North American Free Trade Agreement (NAFTA), a pact signed in 1992 that was meant to gradually eliminate most tariffs and other trade barriers on products and services passing through the United States, Canada, and Mexico. In addition, Chavis was blamed for raising the NAACP's budget deficit. Already high because of declining membership and staff salary increases, the deficit soared to more than $1.2 million.

Finally, in 1994 it was disclosed that Chavis had used NAACP money to pay an out-of-court settlement on a sexual harassment suit filed against him by a female staff member. There were immediate calls for his resignation. On August 20, 1994, in a meeting of the board of directors, Benjamin Chavis was removed as executive director of the NAACP. After his departure, he took an important position in the Nation of Islam and was instrumental in organizing the Nation-sponsored Million Man March in Washington, D.C., that year.

Chavis's stormy tenure and his removal from office highlighted fundamental disagreements among blacks over the primary role of the NAACP in the late 20th century. Full, legal equality having been substantially achieved, the organization faced questions of whether it was prepared to continue offering strong leadership in attacking the problems faced by African Americans.

A turning point came with the naming of Kweisi Mfume as president and chief executive officer on February 15, 1996. Mfume, whose West African name means "conquering son of kings," was born, raised, and educated in the Baltimore, Maryland, area. An activist, organizer, and radio talk-show host, he won a seat on the Baltimore City Council in 1979 by just three votes. During his seven years as a councilman, Mfume led efforts to diversify Baltimore's city government, to improve community safety, to enhance minority business development, and to divest the apartheid government of South Africa of Baltimore city funds. In 1986, Mfume was decisively elected to represent Maryland's 7th Congressional District, a position he held for 10 years. As a member of the House of Representatives, Congressman Mfume advocated landmark minority business and civil rights legislation. He cosponsored and helped pass the Americans with Disabilities Act; authorized the minority contracting and employment amendments to the Financial Institutions Reform and Recovery Act; strengthened the Equal Credit Opportunity Act; and amended the Community Reinvestment Act in the interest of minority financial institutions. He co-authored and amended the Civil Rights Act of 1991 to cover U.S. citizens working for companies abroad. He also sponsored legislative initiatives banning assault weapons and establishing stalking as a federal crime. Mfume served two successful years as chairman of the Congressional Black Caucus and later served as the caucus's chair of the Task Force to Preserve Affirmative Action.

Mfume was unanimously voted into the NAACP presidency by its board of directors. In addition to being the organization's official spokesperson, he assumed responsibility for all daily operations, including fundraising efforts, strategic and financial planning, and supervision of the national staff. Since assuming that position, Mfume has eliminated the organization's debt, raised the standards and expectation of NAACP branches nationwide, and worked with NAACP volunteers across the country to foster a new generation

Kweisi Mfume was unanimously named the president and CEO of the NAACP in 1996. Under Mfume the NAACP has taken great strides toward preparing itself for a successful future.

of civil rights leaders in America. He developed what he calls his five-point action agenda: Civil Rights, Political Empowerment, Educational Excellence, Economic Development, and Youth Outreach. As a result, he has given the NAACP a clear and compelling blueprint for the 21st century.

Before the NAACP can focus solely on the challenges of the new century, however, it must resolve the issues of the 20th century. Among the battles fought by the organization is a lawsuit against gun manufacturers and distributors in an attempt to remove guns from urban streets. The NAACP continues to take on the major TV networks in an attempt to develop initiatives that increase opportunities for

The raising of the Confederate flag at the South Carolina state-house inspired active protest throughout the state, supported and encouraged by the NAACP. The protest proved effective as South Carolina has taken steps recently to change its state flag to both acknowledge its history as a Confederate state and to address concerns from the African-American community.

African Americans in the industry. The organization has imposed economic sanctions on businesses in the state of South Carolina to protest the state's raising of the Confederate flag on federal buildings. It participated in a lawsuit against the Cracker Barrel restaurant chain for what it called "rampant racial discrimination in employment." The NAACP has also attacked the U. S. Supreme Court for its "shameful" record in hiring minority law clerks. A major crisis for the organization concerned the call for an investigation into the NAACP's alleged connection with the Central Intelligence Agency, the Nicaraguan Contras, and Los Angeles, California, gang members.

It is clear that the NAACP has not lost its way in the more than 90 years it has been in existence. The association of more than 2,200 branches and youth councils and nearly a half-million volunteers holds to the belief that racism, sexism, and anti-Semitism cannot and will not be tolerated in American society. For this reason, for nearly a century, the NAACP has been fighting bigotry, which it deems unacceptable and indefensible.

The long and proud history of the NAACP is filled with major accomplishments that have transformed the racial terrain of America. It has improved the lives of millions of citizens, not only African Americans but also whites, Asian Americans, Latinos, and Native Americans. Yet the NAACP firmly believes that the United States is still in desperate need of progressive activists, and it encourages all Americans to participate in its activities and be aware of what still needs to be accomplished. In the words of NAACP president Kweisi Mfume, "The choice many of us face is whether to stand by and watch in the comfort of our own circumstance, or step forward and dare to get involved."

CHRONOLOGY

1905 Black intellectuals and activists organize the Niagara Movement

1908 A race riot in Springfield, Illinois, leads to the founding of the NAACP

1909 The NAACP is founded by Ida B. Wells-Barnett, W. E. B. Du Bois, Henry Moscowitz, Mary White Ovington, Oswald Garrison Villard, and William English Walling

1910 More than 300 blacks and whites meet in New York City for the first NAACP conference; the first issue of *The Crisis* is published by Du Bois

1915 Black migrations begin as thousands of African Americans move to northern cities; the NAACP leads protest demonstrations against *Birth of a Nation;* educator and black leader Booker T. Washington dies

1917 The NAACP wins a legal battle to allow African Americans to be commissioned as officers in World War I

1919 The "Red Summer" race riots hit cities across the nation; black lynchings increase dramatically; the NAACP publicizes the crimes and pushes for antilynching legislation

1920 James Weldon Johnson becomes the first black executive secretary of the NAACP

1931 Roy Wilkins joins the NAACP as assistant secretary

1934 Du Bois resigns his posts at the NAACP; the organization's lawyer, Thurgood Marshall, organizes boycott of Baltimore, Maryland, stores and successfully defends the NAACP after it is sued for the boycott

1939 The NAACP creates the Legal Defense and Educational Fund as a separate organization; Thurgood Marshall is appointed director

1946 The U.S. Supreme Court bans states from having laws requiring segregated facilities in public areas

1954 The U.S. Supreme Court hands down a landmark decision in the *Brown v. Board of Education of Topeka* case, in which segregation in public schools is declared unconstitutional

CHRONOLOGY

1955 Roy Wilkins succeeds Walter White as executive director of the NAACP; NAACP member Rosa Parks helps initiate the civil rights movement by refusing to give up her seat on a Montgomery, Alabama, bus; her arrest leads to a bus boycott protesting the city's segregated seating laws

1957 Congress passes a civil rights act, the first such legislation passed in 82 years

1960 Members of the NAACP Youth Council participate in nonviolent sit-ins in Greensboro, North Carolina, protesting segregated lunch counters

1962 The NAACP heads the battle to desegregate the University of Mississippi by supporting the legal efforts of James H. Meredith

1963 More than 250,000 participate in the March on Washington for Jobs and Freedom; W. E. B. Du Bois dies

1964 Congress passes the Civil Rights Act, preventing discrimination in public accommodations and employment

1965 Congress passes the Voting Rights Act

1972 The U.S. Supreme Court temporarily strikes down the death penalty in *Furman v. Georgia*

1976 Benjamin Hooks succeeds Roy Wilkins as executive director of the NAACP

1981 The NAACP leads efforts to extend the Voting Rights Act for another 25 years.

1984 Hooks leads 125,000 people in a march on Washington to protest the "legal lynching" of civil rights by the Reagan administration

1994 Benjamin Chavis is removed from his position as executive director of the NAACP

1996 Kweisi Mfume is named to replace Chavis as head of the NAACP; Mfume institutes a five-point action agenda encompassing civil rights, political empowerment, educational excellence, economic development, and youth outreach

BIBLIOGRAPHY

Books

Candaele, Kerry. *Bound for Glory: From the Great Migration to the Harlem Renaissance (1910–1930)*. Philadelphia: Chelsea House, 1997.

Chambers, Veronica. *The Harlem Renaissance*. Philadelphia: Chelsea House, 1998.

Duster, Afreda M., ed. *Crusade for Justice: The Autobiography of Ida B. Wells*. Chicago: University of Chicago Press, 1970.

Hauser, Pierre. *Great Ambitions: From the "Separate But Equal" Doctrine to the Birth of the NAACP (1896–1909)*. New York: Chelsea House, 1995.

Hornsby, Alton, Jr. *Milestones in Twentieth-Century Black American History*. Detroit: Visible Ink Press, 1993.

Kellogg, Charles Flint. *NAACP: A History of the National Association for the Advancement of Colored People*. Vol. 1. Baltimore, Md.: Johns Hopkins University Press, 1967.

Klots, Steve. *Ida Wells-Barnett*. New York: Chelsea House, 1993.

Lewis, David Levering. *W. E. B. Du Bois: Biography of a Race 1868–1919*. New York: Henry Holt, 1993.

Loewenberg, Bert James, and Ruth Bogin, eds. *Black Women in Nineteenth-Century American Life: Their Words, Their Thoughts, Their Feelings*. University Park, Pa.: Pennsylvania State University Press, 1976.

Ovington, Mary White. *Black and White Sit Down Together: The Reminiscences of an NAACP Founder*. New York: Feminist Press, 1995.

———. *The Walls Came Tumbling Down*. New York: Arno, 1969.

Salzman, Jack, David Lionel Smith, and Cornell West, eds. *Encyclopedia of African-American Culture and History*. Vol. 4. New York: Macmillan, 1996.

Schroeder, Alan. *Booker T. Washington*. New York: Chelsea House, 1992.

Washington, Booker T. *Up from Slavery*. 1901. Reprint. New York: Viking Penguin, 1986.

Wedin, Carolyn. *Inheritors of the Spirit: Mary White Ovington and the Founding of the NAACP*. New York: John Wiley and Sons, 1998.

Websites:

National Association for the Advancement of Colored People
http://www.naacp.org

National Urban League
http://www.nul.org

W.E.B. Du Bois Institute
http://www.web-dubois.fas.harvard.edu.

Timeline of the American Civil Rights Movement
http://www.wmich.edu/politics/mlk

INDEX

INDEX

INDEX

INDEX

PICTURE CREDITS

page

2: Library of Congress
8: Archive Photos
10: Corbis/Bettmann
16: New York Times Co./Archive Photos
18: Popperfoto/Archive Photos
20: Corbis
23: Hulton Getty Collection/Archive Photos
25: Archive Photos
28: Corbis
33: Corbis
38: Corbis
41: Archive Photos
46: Corbis
48: George Eastman House/ Nikolas Muray/Archive Photos
50: Corbis
52: Corbis
55: Archive Photos
57: Bettmann/Corbis
60: Archive Photos
62: Charles "Teenie" Harris/ Archive Photos
65: Corbis
67: Library of Congress
69: George Tames/ New York Times Co./ Archive Photos
70: Archive Photos
71: Corbis
73: Corbis
75: Archive Photos
76: Express Newspapers/ K955/Archive Photos
79: Corbis
81: Archive Photos
82: Archive Photos
84: Archive Photos
86: Archive Photos
88: Reuters/Joe Giza/ Archive Photos
91: Archive Photos
97: CNP/Archive Photos
98: Corbis

Cover Photos
top: Bettmann/Corbis
middle: Charles A. Harris/Corbis
bottom: Bettmann/Corbis

DARREN RHYM lives in Borgat, Georgia, and teaches English Composition and World Literature at Morehouse College in Atlanta, Georgia. He received his B.A. from Bucknell University in Lewisburg, Pennsylvania, and his M.A. from Pennsylvania State University, in University Park, Pennsylvania. He has published works on numerous subjects, including misogyny in rap lyrics and black images on TV sitcoms. Currently, he is writing a collection of short stories, and is editing autobiographical interviews of Georgians who were born in the early 20th century.